Te' Writes

TURNING A BLIND EYE

SOMETIMES THOSE CLOSEST TO YOU HURT YOU THE MOST

© Copyright 2021 - All rights reserved.

The content contained within this book may not be reproduced, duplicated or transmitted without direct written permission from the author or the publisher.

Under no circumstances will any blame or legal responsibility be held against the publisher or author for any damages, reparation, or monetary loss due to the information contained within this book, either directly or indirectly.

Legal Notice:
This book is copyright protected. It is only for personal use. You cannot amend, distribute, sell, use, quote or paraphrase any part, or the content within this book, without the consent of the author or publisher.

Disclaimer Notice:
Please note the information contained within this document is for educational and entertainment purposes only. All effort has been executed to present accurate, up to date, reliable, complete information. No warranties of any kind are declared or implied. Readers acknowledge that the author is not engaged in the rendering of legal, financial, medical or professional advice. The content within this book has been derived from various sources. Please consult a licensed professional before attempting any techniques outlined in this book.

By reading this document, the reader agrees that under no circumstances is the author responsible for any losses, direct or indirect, that are incurred as a result of the use of the information contained within this document, including, but not limited to errors, omissions, or inaccuracies.

Book Description

What happens when one member of the family decides that the family secret isn't worth keeping?

Based on a true story, this riveting tale exposes the shared secrets that many families would rather take to the grave.

Chantel's world was turned upside-down when she discovered the abuse of her brother Roy at the hands of her mother's boyfriend, J.R. Outrage and panic left Chantel's head spinning. How could someone do something so disgusting and violating?

Even after numerous attempts to end the abuse, Chantel was silenced by her family. It was clear to Chantel that they were not being protected by those who are supposed to love them the most.

The questions lingers with Chantel for years to come: Why is J.R.'s protection continuously held above the love and care of innocent children?

Chantel was expecting that this tortuous situation was in the past. She had hopes that Roy could heal despite of the abusive presence still in their lives. Healing, however, isn't in the cards yet for this family as all three of Roy's children—

Chantel's nieces and nephew—have experienced the same horrors as their father before them. Chantel will not be silent and allow the family to keep J.R.'s sordid secrets.

Turning A Blind Eye introduces a heroine whose fierce ambition has her stop at nothing to expose her family's secret. It is Chantel's mission to reveal the truth and break the generational curse.

TABLE OF CONTENTS

Author Biography vii
Disclaimer viii
Note To The Reader ix
Prologue xi
Chapter 1: Parental Control 1
Chapter 2: Motherhood 12
Chapter 3: A Wolf in Sheep's Clothing 17
Chapter 4: Repercussions 28
Chapter 5: Truth or Lie 37
Chapter 6: Nieces and Nephew 47
Chapter 7: Generational Curse 55
Chapter 8: Spiritual Advisor 63
Chapter 9: Open Clash 72
Chapter 10: Shaken Up 80
Chapter 11: A Promise to Keep 89
Chapter 12: Broken </3 97
Chapter 13: Advice for Parents 112
Chapter 14: Fall Out 124
Chapter 15: After the Storm 136
Epilogue 143
Coming Soon 148
References 149

Author Biography

Te'Writes is an emerging author and founder of the company Posh INK. She grew up in the suburbs of Kansas City but now is living in the metropolis of Denver. You can typically find her enjoying her spare time on a lovely hike on her favorite mountain trails. Te' has always had a passion for writing non-fictional stories that emulate her life experiences. In her debut book, Turning A Blind Eye, she draws from experience from her childhood to write about certain harrowing traumatic events that her main character experiences and conquers. Find out more about Te' and her first non-fictional page-turner at https://tewrites.com/.

SOCIAL MEDIA PLATFORMS :

Disclaimer

This book is a work of nonfiction. However, names and places have been changed in order to protect privacy. Events have been altered or fabricated for the purpose of telling a story. Nothing in this book should be taken as factually accurate except for the cases of child abuse and sexual assault. This story contains heavy content in these themes and may be triggering to some readers. As such, discretion is advised.

NOTE TO THE READER

Dear Reader,

If you have ever experienced sexual abuse or assault in your childhood, this letter is meant for you. I am so sorry this has happened in your life. You were a child. You were young, innocent, and pure. It doesn't matter what clothes you wore, how you walked, thought, spoke, or what you did. You didn't do anything to deserve it. Trust me, it is not your fault. Please do not blame yourself for anything that happened to you in the past. Please do not spend hours questioning the reason it happened to you. Please do not try to make sense of it all because, it doesn't make sense.

I will not ask you to move on; I won't expect that of you. I won't ask you to forget it ever occurred and "fake it 'til you make it." All I want you to do is to take it one day at a time. Sit with yourself. Listen to your feelings. Acknowledge your pain. Let yourself feel the pain. Let yourself cry. Let your heart express itself. Do whatever it is that you think you need to do to make yourself feel better.

It may take some time, but you will rise through this. I assure you, can still heal. You will still find happiness, and you will find the courage to lead your best life. You can find inspiration to pursue your dreams. You will get your confidence back and be able to do everything you wanted to do.

How do I know this? It is because I believe in the power of goodness. I believe in the power of love and time, and I believe that they can both heal you. Hold on tight to this rope of life and there will be light. Believe that you can get through it because you can, not because you have to. You are amazing. You are strong. You are powerful. You can achieve more than you know once you put your mind to it.

Since this book deals heavily with the theme of child abuse and sexual assault, I urge you to be aware of your boundaries and limitations. If this book seems like too much for you, don't force yourself to read it. Take care. Speak to a professional. Seek support. My book is only here to show you the light after such a darkening storm, but in order to see said light, we need to experience the storm. If this makes you uncomfortable, I encourage you to set this book aside. Come back to it when you are ready.

Keep going. I believe in you.

Sincerely,

Te Writes

PROLOGUE

*** Thursday, September 12 ***

My name is Chantel, and sometimes things aren't always what they seem.

I was born at Sky View Medical Center in Kansas City, Missouri, on July 14th, 1980. It's a beautiful place where the weather is always warm, but the winter averages out to around 24ºF. It's quite scenic here.

I've lived in Kansas City all my life. We've got some of the best barbecue, and jazz is a well-known genre heard on our streets. I don't mind it. It helps block out all the noise.

Where we live, isn't the nicest neighborhood filled with the nicest people. Our central community practically swarms with two things: drugs and guns. Usually, it's at the fault of teenagers. A lot of people don't consider it a big deal, particularly because, during the day, it's peaceful and normal.

For every family but ours, that is.

Truthfully, I don't know what normal looks like. I always figured it would have the standard house, enough for everybody in the household—mom, dad, sister, brother. It would have a guest bedroom and all the rooms necessary to live comfortably—a living room, dining room, kitchen. There would be a ground level, top level, and bottom level—whatever. I picture *normal* including a backyard and an elegant front yard, regular nine-to-five day jobs, maybe a dog, too but that isn't at all how it is.

Not for my family at least.

No, my family consists of Mom; my little sister Michelle, who's six years younger than me; and our brother, Roy, two years fresher into life than Michelle. We've all got different dads and none of them are around today except for Michelle's who occasionally takes us all out to have fun. He never leaves me or Roy out whenever he picks up Michelle on the weekends, which is better than anything my dad has ever done. I won't complain even though I wish my dad was here to do the same with me. I'm glad at least one of our fathers includes us.

"Roy's dad, while he's polite and everything, he mainly focuses on Roy. He doesn't necessarily give as much care or attention to me or Michelle. He doesn't bother to involve us in anything more than weekly small talk.

I don't know my dad as well as I always wanted to. I have no idea what he's like. I barely even remember what he looks like. Dad chose to leave when I was only three years old. He didn't want to be in a relationship with Mom, or support her, and Mom did everything she could to keep him away. So, instead, he chose to focus on work—he works as a pastor in a church and he's also a real estate broker in Chicago, Illinois. He grew up in a middle-class home and went to private school kindergarten through twelfth grade.

He's never been broke or poor a day in his life, unlike us. I guess he's always been hardworking in that regard. Maybe that's where I get my work ethic. Since I was the first child, my dad was the first man that Mom fell in love with. He's also the first man that Mom fell out of love with. I guess they've always had opposite views. Dad's always been the driven type, always willing to get things done when they need to be, according to what Mom has told me over the years. Mom is more laid back. She doesn't have a lot of motivation, and when she does, it takes her a long time to finish a job or errand. Regardless, I think they both raised me as well as they possibly could, up until I was three when they finished bringing me up and that was it. They decided to part ways. I haven't seen him since. Sometimes I wonder if Dad were still here, things might've been different for us; that we'd have been in a much nicer neighborhood, gone to much nicer schools, worked better-paying jobs, wouldn't lack money for anything, et cetera. I know I shouldn't really complain, we're doing just fine so far without him after all, but still I wonder.

In the beginning, we stayed in my paternal grandparents' house. I don't remember much of it. All I know is that we moved to Auntie's place, Mom's sister, house soon after. It was the first place I remember growing up and having fun before things changed again. I moved around a lot as a kid, I suppose that's one way to put it. In those days, everything was fine with Mom. I remember playing outside with my friends and neighbors. It was great. I went to school—elementary, middle, and now high school. Life was easy. That is - it was, until Dad found out where we lived.

Mom and Auntie weren't so close anymore. They couldn't resist getting into arguments almost every night—but that wasn't enough to move us someplace else. The truth is Mom didn't want Dad in my life if he wasn't keen on supporting either of us as she wanted. I was too little to understand why. That's what triggered our next move.

We moved here to 5711 Valley High Lane. It's in the heart of the Midwest of Kansas City, MO, packed full of greenery, heat, and local traffic. We'd stayed for nearly a decade, more or less, which is the longest we ever stayed in one house. With all that occurred over the years, I think we could all have been happier someplace else.

Our schools aren't far away, friends are nearby, life is still easy except for Mom's constant bitching and yelling. I would blame it on her lost loves, but I'd known for a long time that it wasn't our lost dads that had been the problem. Mom had been scolding us for years, as long as I can remember. I guess, in a way, those three breakups had been leaving her somewhat torn. I get it, in a way. I know what it's like to be a single parent. But I could do without the verbal maltreatment and manipulation.

Like I said, I'm the first child that Mom ever had, and currently, I'm sixteen years old. Michelle is the middle child, being the second one to hit double digits. Roy is the last, at only eight. That's our version of a normal family - oh, and J.R., he comes around a lot.

There are close neighbors in this environment of poor and lousy housing. J.R. helps Mom out quite frequently, and Mom does the same. He's an older black man, at least in his 30s I'll bet, but I'm not entirely sure. It's not like I care. He's got a full head of dark black hair, deep brown eyes, a rounded nose, and a chiseled jaw. He has an expression of authority on his face all the time. Always. It's like he's used to being in control or manipulative. I don't know. There's something off about him though. I just don't know what it is. Maybe it's the way he gave Mom flowers and barged into our lives, or the way he always looks at me with some sense of admiration in his dark eyes. There's the way he keeps an eye on me and Alexis—my daughter—and sometimes even Michelle and Roy, for that matter, especially Roy. The way he compliments me and gives me and Mom Valentine's Day gifts. It's not that it's necessarily creepy or anything—and he doesn't do it all the time, after all—but it's like he's always watching out for us. But why does it matter? He cares, at least or seems to. He makes Mom happy. I'm just overthinking it. I tend to do that a lot throughout the day, letting my past experiences with men get to my head. That's all I do. Think and think and think, and wonder the whys and the how's of every situation there is. I know how annoying it can get.

"Hey," my friend Christina says, snapping her fingers to break me out of my thoughts. "Is everything okay? You seem a little out of it."

"Huh?" I initially respond, not really aware of what's going on around me. Just drifting. "Yes, I'm fine."

Christina and I have been friends for a few weeks now. We met at lunch when she overheard me complaining about how uptight Mom can be because of an argument we had the night before, of which I don't remember the cause. She said she could relate. Christina's pretty smart and she moved to Kansas City a few months ago. She's got blonde wavy hair and crystal blue eyes that dazzle under any amount of sun we get, and so far, she's been by my side. We're basically milk and chocolate. She's pretty attractive, too. I was surprised to find out she didn't have a boyfriend.

"Come on, you can tell me," She presses. "I know we don't really know each other all that well yet, but I'm here. I want to be here for you if something's going on."

"It's just Travis," I tell her honestly, as if it's no big deal. "We broke up a few days ago."

"Oh, Chantel! I'm so sorry!"

"Don't be," I say with a shrug. "It's Alexis I'm worried about."

"Alexis?" she asks, which reminds me I have yet to tell her about my daughter.

I wave a hand carelessly through the air, signifying that it isn't worth explaining now. Then say, "Don't worry about it. I'll figure it out. I always do."

"Okay, if you say so," Christina says when we come to the intersection. I hit the button to cross the street and go home. Christina raises a hand to tap my shoulder. "Well, I'm going to split for today. See you tomorrow at school, Chantel!"

My hand waves to her back as I watch her go, and soon enough, the light changes to green letting me cross. It's a busy street. There are probably more than a dozen cars waiting, including motorcyclists, bikers, and pedestrians on the other side.

The sun is warm on my face, darkening my skin ever so slightly I raise an arm to block it from my face while I keep moving forward. It's the only direction I can ever go and the only direction I ever will. Still, it's hot. It's hot and uncomfortable and I long to jump in the shower when I get home, but I know that isn't going to happen. I'm far too tired from school. I just want to finish my homework and leave it at that. One last push before calling it a day.

The walk from Oakville Secondary School to home takes a total of six minutes. I pass rows of houses, almost all of them attached and small. Ours is no different. We have a bright green lawn with pretty flowers of different purples, pinks, and shades of blues in the garden. The place has a foundation of stone and the front door matches the garage in chocolate brown. It's good to be home.

After stepping inside and removing my shoes at the door, I'm greeted by Michelle and her friend, Kia, watching television on the living room sofa. It's a standard-sized living room, big enough for both furniture and people with plenty of open room to avoid claustrophobia. The couch, loveseat, and adjacent armchair are gray. Everything is spotless, clean, and put away. Mom isn't home yet, so I know that she's probably still on her way from picking up Roy after school.

I make my way deeper into the house, to the little kitchen, trying not to audibly groan with the fact that Michelle *pretended* to be sick to skip school. I'm sure she did, she looks just fine now compared to how she looked in the morning. There's no way she was sick at all today. Both the living room and kitchen connect with the same ivory walls, only differentiated by the light brown hardwood and white tiles. I make myself a sandwich, spreading peanut butter on one slice and jelly on the other. I have had one every day after school for the past three years. I've developed a preference for the taste.

With my snack, I take my backpack to my room. I know Mom would chastise me for taking food into my room—she's really fussy and paranoid about us leaving messes everywhere—but she isn't home yet. I can finish my sandwich before she returns.

I pull out my notes and my mathematics textbook that I'm borrowing for the semester, and begin my homework. Unlike most people, I like to go to school. Michelle does too, why wouldn't she? She's one of those students who gets straight A's without really trying. Though today she claimed she wasn't feeling well, which I'm certain was a lie. Hell, she was pretty good at acting like she wasn't feeling well this morning. Mom couldn't deny her favorite child the chance to rest. No, of course not. Roy neither, but me? I'm 16, she always reminds me. I should be able to fight through whatever cold or flu I'm feeling. After all, you can't see success by taking too many sick days, right? Even if you hardly take any.

So, I've always been the hardworking student of the family. I do my homework, get good grades, and don't take anything below a B as sufficient. I do enough to get by. Michelle has it easy. Roy and I have to try. And probably worse yet, Michelle always feels the need to rub her perfect grades in our faces. She comes home after test-taking to show off perfect scores in my and Roy's face, and I always roll my eyes at her.

Mom and Roy get home at 3:30 p.m., but with them also comes two other voices. I recognize them as John, Roy's best friend; and J.R., John's dad.

"Michelle, come and welcome J.R. He and John will be staying for dinner," I hear Mom say from downstairs before the front door shuts. "You too, Chantel!"

When I hear her call my name, I pull myself out of my bedroom desk—it's small and a dark oak wood, but enough to hold all of my notes in front of me. I stomp down the stairs and wait at the fifth or so step for them to notice me. Immediately J.R. does, as if he's been waiting for me for hours.

"Hi, J.R.," I greet him unenthusiastically, only keen on returning to my room to finish the last of my homework. J.R. smiles like he always smiles at us. I almost want to vomit. I never really liked J.R.

"Hi there, Chantel," he replies. "Nice to see you looking beautiful as always, I see."

I offer a small smile and say, "Make yourself at home."

Mom leads him to the kitchen and the dining room table. I watch them go through the hallway, past Michelle and Kia, and sit before I retreat back to my room to finish my homework.

By the time Mom calls us all for dinner, it's 6:46 p.m. We wash up and take seats. The dining room consists of all polished wood, a deep brown table, and ten matching chairs. Mom sits at one end of the square table like she always does, and J.R. sits beside her on her right. I have no doubt that they're holding hands under the table. Michelle sits at Mom's other side and Roy sits next to her. I, unfortunately, get to sit right next to J.R. and his son, John, because it would be rude of me to sit on the other side so far away from everyone. I try not to roll my eyes at the thought. Alexis is in her high chair beside me, and I feed her from her own kid's plate of rice, mashed potatoes, peas, and boiled cheesy cauliflower.

I hate it when J.R. has dinner with us. Even more so, I hate to see Mom and him hold hands. I don't know if they're really dating or anything. Neither of them has mentioned anything of the sort, but for some reason, it gets to me. I just don't trust J.R. and I don't want to see Mom get her heart broken again.

I try not to look up at him while I eat. I just try to focus on my own dish and Alexis. Today's dinner consists of yellow rice, peas, potatoes, broccoli, and meatloaf. Mom is always sure to put tons of care and attention into the meals she makes. There isn't ever a time that we eat plain leftovers from the fridge. She always has a way of turning something old into something new. I envy that. I'd be far too lazy to put that much detail into meals.

"So, how was school, girls?" Mom asks while the table is silent. "Are you feeling better, Michelle?"

"Much better, Mom," Michelle answers, and I roll my eyes at that. She sees me do it, but decides not to comment. "Thanks for asking."

"What about you, Chantel?" Mom asks again, and I snap to attention.

"Good, Mom," I reply. "Passed my last math test."

"That's great," she says and continues to eat her dinner. I don't bother with explaining my grade or how I should've gotten a higher one but didn't because of the teacher's stubbornness. I know Mom doesn't care much, as long as the grade is good. "Anyway, I've been meaning to tell all of you."

Only then do I look up from my plate.

"Tell us what, Mom?" asks Roy.

Mom looks at J.R. and J.R. looks back at her. They both smile until J.R. speaks. "I was thinking of moving in."

"Moving in?" I repeat aloud, confused as to when, how, and most importantly why he wants to move in with us. I just don't like the idea of seeing them together 24/7.

J.R. nods. John seems to beam with glee. "It was my John's suggestion," J.R. explains, "and I figure, since we come over here often, why not? Your mother seems okay with it, isn't that right?"

Mom smiles like they've had this discussion before. "That's right," she responds.

For a moment, there is silence around the table, none of us quite sure of what to say or how to react. I swear I can even hear the old grandfather clock ticking away in the living room across the house. Mom and J.R. continue watching each other and holding hands under the table.

They must think I don't know, but I can see the way their shoulders and forearms extend. I grit my teeth but don't let it show.

"When?" I ask, neither happiness nor unhappiness in the tone of my voice.

"Hm?" asks Mom inattentively.

"I mean, when are they moving in, Mom?" I ask, slight annoyance edging into my sound. "Do you know, or did you not bother to ask for that detail?"

"Oh, uh, maybe in the next year or so," J.R. guesses, keeping his eyes on Mom to see if she agrees or disagrees. "I don't think you have anything to worry about right now, Chantel. It will take some time to prepare and plan for, longer than you might think."

That at least lets the tension in my shoulders lessen. I'm glad I don't have to worry about it now, but I still can't help but think of the possibility of J.R. calling me *sweetheart* in the future, as if he's about to play the part of our new father figure. I groan internally.

"Yes," Mom replies. "That sounds perfect."

Chapter 1:
Parental Control

After dinner, I help Mom with tidying up the dishes, which basically accounts for rinsing and stacking them neatly in the dishwasher. Then, I take Alexis from her highchair and get her ready for bed; bath, diaper change, and all. Once she's set for bed, I feel that same old tiredness kick in as I place her in the crib in my room. It's small and a pristine white filled with teddies and animal plushies. I sing her a typical lullaby like I always do until she falls asleep, and when she does, I shower myself under warm soapy water and change into my pajamas.

All is quiet behind Michelle's and Roy's doors, but a slight ruffling comes from Mom's bedroom. I don't want to think about what she and J.R. are doing inside there.

With the rest of my homework done, I tidy up my desk and pile my books into my purple school bag. Then, I hop into bed, grab the book I'm reading from my shelf, and call it a night. It is 11:34 p.m. by the time I put it aside.

Thankfully, Alexis doesn't wake up crying like she usually does. It's a peaceful night except for the hollow and distant whispers of Mom and J.R. Somehow I'm able to figure out that this is a dream.

In a vast void of space and emptiness, I can hear them. They are both chasing me down our neighborhood street as if they are some kind of serial hunters, predators, or a form of sin. They're fast and they gain on me. They shout words that I can't hear in the dead of night. I pass people on the streets, however few of them there are. What are they doing out here if it's night? I don't know why they're chasing me? I think I try to tell them to stop, that it isn't funny, that I'm too tired to deal with this. I duck into alleys behind a row of houses, I try and evade them in a trash can, but it's like they have eyes on me all the time, always. I can never rest knowing that they'll find me next time. At one point, they pull me out from under a mound of trash and a thrown away mattress. I see the barrel of a gun in J.R.'s hand seconds before it fires. It's a simple pistol like many people carry in our neighborhood. I hear its bang before I can stop it, not that I ever can, just that I hope to.

Then, I wake up.

In the morning, my alarm clock beeps to signify the start to another school day. I breathe heavily like I've just finished a run on the track outside Oakville's football field. I don't usually get nightmares, but this was a weird one—aren't they all? I find myself questioning where I have been all night. Why were they chasing me? Was it night or day? If it was night, why were there people on the streets? It probably doesn't matter. I rub the sleep from my eyes.

It's Thursday, my busiest day. I've got school until 3 p.m. With a presentation at 1:30 on the topic of political history, work till 6:30 p.m. As always, I have to take care of Alexis or make sure someone is taking care of her through it all.

After a shower to wash away the sweat and dread from the nightmare, I finish dressing and applying just the right amount of makeup to make my natural features pop. Alexis stirs as I pull her out of the crib and bring her downstairs. I feed her breakfast, change her and hand her off to mom. I grab my backpack, and head off to school. I am always sure that I look as amazing as the day before, if not more so. It's one of the few areas that I can make perfect in my messy life.

"Good morning, Jessica." I greet a friend at the big yellow building when I run into her at the main entrance. There are people of all grades between ninth and twelfth already making their way inside. "What's up?"

"Oh, hey, Chantel!" she shouts back excitedly. "The sky, obviously. How are you?"

"Eh, not bad, you know, considering everything that's going on," I reply.

"Of course, of course," she says. "Travis?"

"Yup," I say. Jess and I have been good friends since childhood. We've known each other since we were six years old. Ever since she moved to the Midwest Jess has been one of my best friends. "Doesn't seem like he's coming back, just like her Grandad."

"Hey, cheer up," Jess pleads, patting my shoulder. "I'm sure Alexis won't mind. I mean, kids aren't supposed to be able to remember things when they're so young. You can keep her missing dad out of the picture if you really want to."

I give Jess a look, one that tells her how ridiculous she's being right now. That isn't me, and it never will be me. I know she isn't being all that serious. We've known each other for so long, way longer than I've known Christina, so I'm not mad at her. Still, she's confused at my expression.

"I'm not my mom, Jess," I explain to her then. "I won't lie to Alexis when she's older about why her dad isn't with her. I don't want that for her. I'd rather just tell her the truth when she's old enough to understand."

Jess just shrugs and flips a short strand of her black bob-cut hair. "Whatever you fancy, Chantel. I know you can handle it." Jess is good like that. She knows human psychology fairly well. It's in her family heritage and she's a bit of a geek in that regard. She knows how genuine and honest I like to be, even if everybody around me claims it's better to lie.

Together, we head inside and stop by our lockers to organize ourselves for our first classes. Our lockers are situated on the second floor and about 30 feet apart from one another.

Once we have our books and binders, it's off to math class which, thank God, Jess and I share. The morning starts out rough, and with science right after, compounding my frustration. Sometimes, I wonder how the people in student services downstairs make these combinations to begin with, as if they purposely do it to give us hell. Jess makes things easier. She's good at math and sometimes helps me out with the questions. We support each other in times of need and never cheat. Math, to us, is simply repetition and practice. That's all we do, and occasionally we quiz each other too.

In my next class, Jessica and I part ways. I head to science class while she heads to philosophy, a class I wouldn't dare try to take on. Today, we're focused on the chemistry section of science since it's our first unit of the course. If I weren't okay with doing the work, I'd probably feel completely suffocated. It's university level. All of my classes are, not that I need it. The truth is that I'm not entirely sure what I should be doing, if I even need a university English or math or science grade of 90% or higher. I don't really care either way. I just do what I have to do to get by. I guess I've always carried an attitude of "deal with it when you have to."

By the time our lunch break arrives for eleventh graders, I meet the rest of my friends in the school cafeteria, which is busy at any lunch period of the day, whether it's the nines, tens, or twelves. We all talk about whatever bullshit is going on in our lives. I suppose that involves Travis too.

"Fuck him," says Skyla, the dark uncaring one that resorts to her "give zero fucks" attitude whenever things start to look the worst. "Thank God you dumped him, Chantel." We all laugh at that, all four of us knowing it was the other way around; Jess, Skyla, Kassandra—the lightly tanned princess of us all—and myself.

"Okay, but Alexis won't be happy with me," I reply, a little less gleeful than my friends.

"It's all good," Kassie says easily. "She'll adapt, girl! Don't take it too harshly!"

"Yeah, I guess you're right."

"Anyway…" Jess says, lulling the word over to shift our focus gently. "How is Alexis doing, Chantel? I haven't seen her in forever."

"Oh, she's fine," I reply initially. "Sounds great."

"You should totally bring her to class at some point!" Skyla urges, and I shake my head at that, not at all for the first time. Skyla is probably the most sly and devious of us all. Kind and friendly on the outside, but once you get to know her, she can be quite rebellious. Ever since I had Alexis, she's been begging me to bring her to school and show her off, but I can't.

"It's against school policy, Skyla," I tell her again, annoyed but gentle at the same time. "You know that."

"Oh, loosen up," she reprimands. "Who cares?"

I do. Though I would never admit that to any of them— except Jess of course because I'm pretty sure she already knows. I don't like to come off as much of a show-off or rebel.

Once we finish lunch, we head to our afternoon classes. I've got political history and, for once, I feel semi-ready for the presentation I have to give. Usually, history wouldn't be my go-to in terms of subjects to select for school, and it's not that everything else was taken. I know there were plenty of others to choose from, but I just saw the course and thought there was no harm in trying something new. I took history last year, which was boring as hell to get through, but political history? I can't deny that it caught my eye.

The assignment was to research one of the United States' most popular political leaders over time and explain to the class what made them a leader, why they became a leader, and how they came out of power in the White House. I did my presentation on George H.W. Bush, the president from 1989-1993. I go into thorough detail explaining his successes and setbacks, goals and motivations, history, and the context of the time period he was in power—which wasn't all that long ago—and I end with one of his most popular quotes. "Any definition of a successful life must include service to others."

I complete my presentation precisely nine seconds before exceeding the time limit. It was supposed to be at least ten minutes long and no more than fifteen.

When I finish, everyone claps, like they usually do. The class consists of approximately 21 students, including me. Usually, I'd be nervous if I hadn't prepared ahead of time. Today, I was confident. I worked my ass off for this, and I had no doubt I'd receive a good mark for it.

"Well done, Chantel," notes Mr. Wellish, the only political history teacher in Oakville Secondary School. He is an older man, dark skin tone but not too dark with a head that's slowly going bald, his gray hair still lasting at the edges. He's tall, probably around six foot four with a skinny build. "Have a seat."

I nod and oblige, heading back to my desk that is all of two rows from the front. I sit behind Cameron, one of the most popular boys in school. His head is down on his desk. He always naps during Mr. Wellish's class.

A few other classmates perform their presentations on Abraham Lincoln and John F. Kennedy. I tune out what they say about their findings after half the class goes by, not by choice, just by lack of excitement in their voices. All of a sudden, I'm counting myself lucky enough to have a teacher for a class like this with a fresh voice every class and an engaging attitude. Mr. Wellish wasn't boring or dull in the slightest. If I were to have a teacher with a monotonous voice, I know I wouldn't last long enough to get a good grade.

Gym class is the easiest round of the day and the last. It requires little to no intellect or mental functioning, nothing but acting on instinct.

I guess I'm not so good at that. I'd rather do homework than run laps, but today, we're doing just that.

We ran five warm-up laps around the gymnasium perimeter before Ms. Allegro takes us outside on the football field to play a game of soccer. The gym wasn't all that big, but it wasn't small either. It likely covers at least 100 feet in length and 50 feet in width. It's painted with lines matching our school colors orange and green. One line along the outside court, another running a few feet inside of it, and the last creating a circle in the center.

At the time of everyone completing their warm-up, Ms. Allegro explains how soccer is a common sport worldwide, but is most culturally appreciated in Brazil. Most of the class already knew the rules of soccer. No touching the ball with your hands, only feet, scoring in the other net (though we're only using half of the football field instead of the whole length), two teams, no trash-talking. She splits us up and we play. It's straightforward stuff, and part of me wonders if she's only having us play for physical activity and because she couldn't fit anything else into her "lesson plan."

We don't keep score. We just play to have fun. All the while, Ms. Allegro shouts terrible puns at us on the sidelines or reminds us to pass along to other teammates. I try to block her out, but she continues to be a hell of a distraction.

When school is over and she dismisses us, I don't waste any time. I gather my things and head home to take care of Alexis; change her, feed her, love her. Me and Mom, we could only ever afford a babysitter between the hours of 9 a.m. to 12 p.m., which is great because for the few hours that Mom works as a public transit supervisor, she is able to both help me out with Alexis and keep her home. It works because I'll be working late today.

I work at the local call center as a customer service representative, which is a place where people can make enquiries about other companies. My job is to answer their questions or direct them to someone who can. It isn't far from our house, about a ten-minute walk. I get changed into my work clothes and walk the few blocks.

There aren't many people that call during the later hours of the day. It's mostly just cataloging and organizing calls that we've been given at the start and answering any that come up. Most of the people sound older, speak with a heavy African American accent, or are just impolite. They curse about the company they're complaining about to me and my few coworkers that work late at night. It doesn't bother us as much as it used to.

Tonight, I'm working alone with my manager, Dave, until 10 p.m. He's an older white man, scrawny with a thick head of dark hair and a clean face. He has to be somewhere in his fifties at least. "Hey, Chantel," he states. "Got quite a few calls earlier between 9 and 11. Let's get them logged into our database, please."

"Sure thing," I reply and begin to go through the day's calls. It turns out, there are a lot to go through, at least 30 of them listed on the computer screen. Sometimes I wonder why the call center even bothers to categorize them. It seems pointless. We hardly ever use the past numbers anyway, not to my knowledge at least, but I learned from experience that sometimes it's best to keep a record of things.

For the most part, this is all I do, that and welcoming and responding to any customer calls that come in. Some are probably just looking for a chance to rant about their bad experiences with a company from whom they purchased. Others sound as if they've been personally offended by the employees. Ninety percent sound impolite or jocular, as if they're drunk.

It's times like these when I think about Dad the most. Even though this line of work is nothing like I imagine a Christian pastor's job is meant to be. Those sorts of people feel somehow relatable, like they need support, a prayer answered from God, a light in their darkness. I don't know what any of these customers are looking for outside of a quick rant or a piece of justice, but there's something about them that makes me deeply miss him. I hardly even knew my dad, but still. Maybe it's the distant sound in these people's voices or the drag of their anger. Perhaps it's the attitude or the dialect they speak. There's something, especially thanks to Dave.

Dave always wears a Christian cross on his shirt, always keeping it visible to anyone that might see. It's small, simple, one straight line intersecting the other. If there's one detail I remember about Dad, it's a similar looking cross that kept hanging out of his shirt day in and day out. He wore it constantly and had it for as long as I can remember, maybe longer. The most upsetting part about that is I know nothing else about him and he knows nothing about me. He knows nothing about Alexis.

Mom never wanted Dad around. That's the reason he hasn't been in my life. Mom did everything she could to keep him away and I don't blame her. To be fair, it's mostly on Dad, not Mom. Dad could've chosen to put more effort into our family than he did, but he chose not to. All he did was pay child support. I know because I would find the checks whenever I would go to pick up our mail. That's all. Dad never did anything else. I know I shouldn't be complaining. After all, Roy and Michelle's dads don't even do that, but at least their dads were somewhat present.

I shake my head. *Why are you doing this to yourself, Chantel?* I think to myself. *Just because you lost Dad, that means you lost Travis and every man's love? No, that can't be.* I try to make myself believe it but the more

I think about it, the more I believe it's true. I cannot fathom comprehending that when Alexis is old enough to understand, she'll never know her grandad and dad just like I don't. I really wanted a better life for her than what I had. I really did, but what if that's impossible?

Alexis and I are staying in the same place as I've always stayed, a poor and unsafe neighborhood that feeds off of crime and dirtbags with little income, men that can't provide or understand, and an inexperienced mom to call her own. Sometimes I'm not sure which way is forward.

How am I supposed to deal with that? How am I supposed to change Alexis's future without having much to use? What am I supposed to do?

Mom isn't helpful. Maybe she is on the physical side of raising a child, but nowhere close to the emotional side or the planning. Michelle and Roy are still young. I can't get them any more involved than they already are. They don't deserve to be looped into my problems. They should be having fun while they can. So, without Dad, I'm on my own and I don't know how to change anything. I don't know.

I just don't know.

Chapter 2:
Motherhood

> *"It doesn't matter who you are, or where you are from. The ability to triumph begins with you—always."*
>
> —Oprah Winfrey.

Raising a daughter isn't all that easy, especially for a sixteen-year-old. I had Alexis last year, March 16, 1996. She is almost a year and a half old at this point and I love her more than anything. It isn't just her smooth, jet-black hair or the twinkle in her chestnut brown eyes. There's a softness to her brown skin and a gentleness to the way she grasps my finger whenever I come home from a late shift at work. It's 11:39 p.m. and she doesn't want any sleep tonight. The way she always smiles and clings to me when I pick her up and she giggles when I nudge her nose with mine— I just know she's mine and she always will be, and there's something totally and uniquely pure about it.

It's what I imagine it's like to stare into heaven or brush an elbow against an earthy plant full of life and energy.

I'd do anything for my little Alexis if I could; gifts, parties, infinite playtimes, moving to a safer environment or getting our own place. However, I can't. My income is far too low, and until I finish secondary school at Oakville and university hopefully very soon, I will be able to make more money. Besides, that could take a while.

Mom helped a lot, more than I ever could have expected her to. I didn't ask her to look after Alexis while I'm in school, but she did anyway. She deserves more credit than I give her. Ever since Dad left, I've been wondering how I was going to be able to raise a kid on my own and so young. Mom and Dad weren't so much older than me when they had me. It hurts to think that Alexis's dad left earlier than mine did, and worse still to think that she won't really know her dad or granddad. It's something that I've always been hoping for, to be able to see Dad again, but I never wanted Alexis to grow up hoping the same thing. I wish things could be different between us, between all of us. Not just me, but Michelle and Roy and Mom. I want a better life for Alexis than I have. I really do.

When she begins to stir in my arms, I rock her while moving back to my bed. I sit down on the edge of the soft mattress and cradle her, rock her side to side, from left to right, right to left, gently and alluringly.

I'm not a heavy sleeper which sucks because any little noise wakes me up just as easily as a fire alarm would. Alexis' crying is no different. I'm always able to tell when she needs me. Part of me wonders if that's motherly instinct or if it's really just me being a light sleeper and easily attentive whenever my darling cries this late at night.

"Shh," I whisper to her, giving her a pacifier to soothe her. It's a light soft pink, but with the little light from the bedside lamp beside us, it looks darker than it is. It always seems to help to some degree, and tonight is the same. "Hush now, sweetie, don't say a word. Listen to Mama's voice now. I've got you."

I start to hum and sing the lullaby I always sing to her whenever she can't fall asleep. I do so in the quietest voice imaginable, but not so low she can't hear me. I sing slowly and deliberately so little baby Alexis can pay attention to each sound. She's in the process of learning her first words and can already say "Mama." I always talk to her at night.

When I finish getting through our usual lyrics, I hum the tune for a little longer while getting up and returning her to her crib. I pull the soft white blanket over her, hand her the teddy she always sleeps with, and lean over the crib's bars watching her drift off again. I'm interrupted with a yawn, but otherwise finish my humming lullaby just a few seconds after she closes her eyes.

There isn't a day or night that I will complain about waking up to Alexis' cries. There's not a day or night I can complain about holding her longer than is necessary. Even though I'm extremely tired from a full day of school and a busy evening of work, I wouldn't throw away a single minute to spend with Alexis. Though, what gets to me is that homework has a habit of interfering with our interactions.

It's one of the things I hate most about being a teenage mom. There are far too many things I need to be aware of constantly when that could wait until I'm older. I'm in high school, which means I'm still trying to get good grades and make it to some college or university so I can get a degree of some sort. I'm not like Michelle. I can't just not study and end with As. It doesn't come that easy to me.

I have my and Alexis' future to worry about. We're still living under Mom's roof, so I guess that's a lucky break, but I still need to think about after, and where we're going to live when Alexis grows older. I want her to have her own home while she's growing up just like I did. I don't want us to stay with Mom forever. I want her to see me as independent and able to look after her as a good parent. I don't want to have to live on government benefits like Mom does or have to rely on men like J.R. for financial support. I don't want to have to ask for help from anybody.

With my future also comes my career. I need to make sure I'm doing something in the future to make enough money to support us. Right now, work at the call center is enough, but eventually it won't be. That's what makes me nervous. If I don't find a way to get out of it and get something more lucrative, then I don't know what I'm going to do after I graduate from Oakville, where I'm going to go, or how to fulfill Alexis' life to the best of my ability.

It's these sorts of things that keep me up at night. It's not that I suffer from insomnia or anything, I don't. Sometimes I just really wish I hadn't paired up with Travis. He is just like all the other men in Oakville, selfish and ambivalent, not to mention that he's always been a womanizer. As young as we both were, he couldn't stand to not interact and engage with multiple girls, from school and elsewhere. I hate that I was just one of them. He might not be as selfish as other people, but he does care more for himself than all the girls he sleeps with. I just never found out how much he lacked in personality until we had Alexis.

I told him that if he couldn't commit, or better yet, commit to me and Alexis—then it would probably be best if we parted ways. I still remember his response that day.

"I can't have Alexis and not you, Chantel!"

I didn't care. So, I contributed to ending things on my own terms. I didn't give him a chance to prove himself or dump all the other girls he was involved with. I was done with him. I didn't want him as a dad for Alexis anyway. God knows he'd probably be horrible at it. He was there with me when Alexis came, and thank God for that. I didn't want to do it alone, but it wasn't long after that I realized how much I didn't want him anywhere near her. I didn't need him.

I lay in bed easily on my left side, remembering all that I had with him and thinking of how better off I am now. I don't care if he wants to forget about Alexis. He can forget about me or her all he wants. I don't care. I know it'll be better if he isn't here.

Eventually, my eyes get heavy with a new tiredness. The last time I looked at the clock, it read 1:19 a.m., and the last thing that I think is how glad I am that our relationship didn't last. As sorry as I am for Alexis that she'll likely never know her father, I also think it's for the best. Then, I drift.

Chapter 3:
A Wolf in Sheep's Clothing

~ Roy ~

"Hey, Roy!" John calls out when Mom and J.R. get to the fence outside of Oakville Elementary School. It's a division off of Oakville Secondary School, which is where Chantel and where Michelle is going to go when she turns 15. "Do you want to come over to my place after school?"

I look up at Mom, wondering if she will let me go. She smiles down at me and I know that means yes. "Sure, Roy," she says like always. "Go have fun."

She takes my navy blue backpack from my shoulders and hangs one of the straps off her own, and with that I'm able to run along much faster and easier. John doesn't bother to ask J.R. to carry his red and black backpack. He just carries it on his back the entire walk home.

"Yay! Thanks, Mama!" I shout in reply. Then, I look at John, who waits for me, "Let's go!"

It's a nice warm day today. There are no clouds in the sky. It's as clear as a vast desert of scorching hot sand, but not as hot as one. The temperature probably barely reaches over 77 degrees. It's my favorite type of weather, not too hot and not too cold. It even has a slight wind blowing through my dark brown hair, making it a mess, but I don't care. It's a perfect day for shorts and a t-shirt, and I'm glad I'm wearing exactly that.

John and I run off ahead, past Mom and J.R. and further along the cement path that we always take to get home. It's a path through the trees, and we always run along the edge of it, brushing our hands against the tops of bushes and leaves. We pass a bunch of other school kids walking the path with their parents. Some of them wave, smile, join us, or all three.

Eventually, we made it back home. We hear Mom and J.R. talking and laughing behind us. John and I do too, all the way until we get to our front yard— the yard where the grass is always green no matter how hot it is, greener than all the neighbors', and the flowers are always pretty because Mom always takes good care of them. Mom's silver SUV is in the driveway and she waves to us on the porch.

"I'll see you at seven for dinner, Roy!" she shouts at me.

I shout back happily, "Okay!"

Then, John and I follow the street up to J.R.'s place. It is only a few doors away. All of the houses on our street look more or less the same. Each house is attached to another house with one garage, a small front yard and porch, two floors, and a basement. I bet the backyards are about the size as the front yards too. That's what it's like for most of them.

J.R.'s black four-seater is in the driveway of his home. It doesn't have a white plate on the back or front of it. I'm not sure why, but I never bother to ask. I already know J.R. doesn't really like to talk about himself. Besides, it doesn't bother me. I just want to get inside or outside and practice my rap dance with John.

"Are you boys hungry?" J.R. asks when we go inside. It's almost the same as Mom's but smaller and meant for no more than two people. It's probably about twice as small, but the layout is basically the same.

The living room is on the left when you come in with a kitchen connected to it, stairs on the right, a bathroom next to it, and a hallway from the door leading to the backyard. I've been here countless times. I know where everything is as well as John or J.R. do. Plus, I've slept over dozens of times.

"No thanks, Dad," John answers, and I shake my head.

John asks if we can go outside to the backyard to practice our newest rap, and J.R. says to go ahead, so we do. Their backyard isn't that much smaller than ours. It's square and simple with a small stone patio with easy-to-use chairs and a small round table in the center. John and I mostly practice out on the grass. There's freshly cut grass. I don't think J.R. even cuts it himself. He looks too old even if he wanted to cut it by himself, but Mom has always told me not to say that in front of him. I never want to be rude. Also, the entire yard is fenced off with wooden planks. Some parts of it are old and rotten and look like they will fall over, but they never do. It's completely sectioned off from the other neighbors beside and ahead on the other street. The whole area is probably 100 feet across and 80 feet out from their house like ours. It's not a bad backyard. It's pretty enough.

We've been following rapper's songs and copying their routines for years. John and I both like to dance along with them. We listen to the beats, to the rhythm, to the music, and sing to the words like they're ours. We know almost every song by heart and can perform them perfectly. MC Hammer, 2Pac, and Master P. are just a few of our favorites to act out, especially "Dear Mama" by 2Pac and "Stop Hatin" by Master P., but "U Can't Touch This" by MC Hammer and "Ice Baby" by Vanilla Ice have always been long time favorites. It was one of the first songs we listened to.

J.R. lets John use his phone all the time whenever we go to practice together and match our movements at the same time. Mom calls it synchronization, I think, whatever that means. She says even though we're only eight, we could be in the school talent show performing our rap dances for the entire school. Me and John always laugh and do crazier dances to prove her wrong.

We don't really care for dancing along to the songs in front of anybody, but we aren't shy if anyone does watch us either. We mostly do it to have fun. We're not into impressing anybody, but it's great if we can make them laugh, like Mom does when we act out more crazily than we mean to. That's on purpose, and she does always laugh when she sees us do it.

As soon as John puts the music on, we line up beside each other and get ready to jump at the first beat of the drum. From there it's just easy movements. Sometimes we mess up and one of us trips and falls down to the grass. It doesn't hurt because we're used to it, but it stops our flow and we have to start over again. Usually, it's John that always slips up, and he gets upset when he does. I just make sure he knows it's fine and that there's no big deal about starting over again.

"Hey, it's fine," I always tell him and offer him my hand to help him up faster. "The more we retry it, the better we get at the other sections. C'mon, let's try it again."

Once, twice, three times, four. We only mess up a couple of times for each song that we know and more for the ones that are brand new and fresh in our heads. We never miss a beat and we never fumble more than ten times in a song. Sometimes we even sing along to the lyrics, only censoring ourselves when a swear word comes up, and sometimes we just dance along to the flow of the beat and the rhythm. We have almost every song practiced, memorized, and perfected.

At 5:15, we take a break because John says he needs to use the bathroom. So, he goes inside and I sit on one of the chairs under the old gray gazebo.

It isn't long until the back door opens, and I look up to see J.R. stepping out with a jug of lemonade and two tall glasses on a tray. He usually brings us some kind of snack or juice to enjoy midway through practicing. Sometimes it's apple juice or grape juice, crackers and cheese, or fruit and nuts.

"Are you thirsty?" he asks, and I nod. Lemonade is one of our regular cool drinks that John and I always go for whenever we finish a routine or take a break. He puts the tray on the small round table in front of me and pours the lemonade from the jug into the two glasses. One for me and one for John, filled almost to the rim. He hands it to me when he's done and I thank him with a gentle nod of my head, like I always do.

"So, how's the routine coming along?" J.R. asks.

"Good," I tell him plainly with a smile on my face. I add, "We're having fun."

J.R. smiles, sitting in a similar single chair a little way away from me on my right. "I'm glad to hear that. You looked good when you were doing it together, at least from what I saw when I was inside."

"You were watching us?" I wonder and smile. I laugh, a little embarrassed to find out he'd been watching us.

"Of course I was!" J.R. replies. "I love watching you two dance along to the music. Are you boys going to keep going when Johnny comes back?"

"Yeah!" I shout excitedly, and he smiles.

For a time we just sit quietly, J.R. doesn't say anything else. I just listen to the pretty birds sing in the trees while sipping my lemonade, waiting for John to come back so we can keep practicing the latest song by Master P.

The lemonade is sour and cold, but not enough to stop drinking it or let it warm up. It's refreshing and I drink it little by little, sip by sip.

Eventually, J.R. stands up again. I think he's going to go inside again, maybe get something else or ask John where he is, but he doesn't. He comes closer to ruffle my hair. I lean back, duck, and laugh away from him.

"You're a cute kid for your age, Roy, you know that?" he says, and I smile.

"Mom says that all the time."

"Yes, but I think you're more adorable than she realizes."

He moves behind me and I feel him rub his hands over my shoulders, like they hurt, but they don't. He rubs my shoulders and up my neck. I feel his hands over my smooth skin, they're older and bigger and rougher. At first it tickles a bit, like there's an iciness to his fingers, then that feeling goes away.

I lean forward to keep his fingers off of my skin, but they just come forward with me again and stay. "Don't be shy, Roy," J.R. says quietly to me, and edges closer to sit on the armrest of my seat.

J.R. is an older man. I don't think he works anymore, not for a while at least, and I don't know where he worked before. I never really saw him as that kind of person. I don't know why. He was just always there to pick up John from school, and sometimes me too when Mom couldn't. They would take turns like that. Usually, they both come to pick us up from the side fence. Sometimes J.R. would show up alone, and sometimes Mom showed up alone. They would stay with us both until the other one could come take us home, whichever place we were staying in after school at the time. J.R. barely looks over 50 years old. His hair is just starting to gray at the sides, but from a distance it's hard to tell. It still looks dark black. He is tiny compared to other men in Kansas City, without big arms or a wide chest, and he never has hair on his face. His chin and mustache are always clean.

"I'm not shy," I say, wanting to prove him wrong and sit up a little straighter. So, I shout and point a thumb at myself proudly, smiling wide, "I'm never shy!"

"Well then, what's with the takeback?" J.R. questions, and I have nothing to say to that. I just sit quietly, still, holding my glass in my lap.

After what feels like a few minutes passed, J.R. just takes hold of the top of my glass, takes it from my hand, and puts it back on the table.

Then, he kneels in front of me, resting a dark hand on my knee. "Just relax, Roy. Let it happen. Come on, you know me."

"Let what happen?"

As if in response, he runs his bare hand from my ankle up my leg, to my knee, to my thigh, then to my waist. I want to get up and go find John. I wonder what's taking him so long, but J.R. is in the way. There isn't enough room for me to do so, and I don't exactly want to just tell him to move. That isn't polite. I don't know what to do.

I wish Mom was here. I don't like how close he is all of a sudden, and I don't know how to tell him that without hurting his feelings and being rude. I wish Mom was here to take me home. I want to go home now. I don't want to dance or practice with John anymore. I just want to go home, but I don't know what to do.

The backdoor slides open, and John steps out with a half-eaten cookie. I look at him while J.R. is still close, still watching me close, and J.R. eventually does too.

"Ah, Johnny! My boy!" J.R. says then, stretching his arm out to him and off of me. "Come here, son."

John does, holding and crunching on the last few bites of the chocolate chip cookie in his hand, he walks into his dad's arms.

"Roy is feeling a little shy about me," he tells John. "How's about you explain to him that there's nothing to worry about, hm?" John smiles at J.R., nods happily, then smiles at me. He sits on his dad's knee while they both stay down in front of me. J.R. holds John tightly around his small waist and kisses his cheek.

"I'm not shy…" I say again, but this time my voice is quieter than before.

"Then what's the matter?" John asks, and for some reason that upsets me. What is that even supposed to mean? Does John know what his dad is talking about? Does he know what J.R. just did? Has J.R. been that close or touched him like he just touched me?

Maybe that's normal for them, though. Maybe J.R. is right. Maybe there's nothing to worry about. Why am I worrying anyway? I've known John and J.R. since I was six. They are like family to us. So, why does this feel so weird?

"Nothing," I say to John. "Nothing's the matter. It's just—"

"Just what?" J.R. presses and puts a hand on my lap before he moves it up my arm. I don't notice the way my feet shuffle to the side, to the left, away from them.

At 7 p.m., J.R. and John walk me home. When we get there, I head straight to my room and shut the door. I hate everything about what J.R. did today.

I was having a normal day. John and I were just having fun, dancing to our favorite songs, until he came over. It all felt weird, and I hated it from minute one. I hated it so much. I just wanted Daddy. I wanted my daddy to come home. Even though I never really knew him, saw him, or remembered him at all, I didn't want Mom or Michelle or Chantel or friends or John or J.R. I just wanted my *real* daddy. I still want my real daddy. I don't care if Mom doesn't love me. I know she doesn't. She would never let that happen to me if she did and it's her fault that he did that. I hate both of them.

The more J.R. touched me and rubbed my arm, legs, thighs, skin, the more it felt weird. I didn't like it. I don't know why I didn't, I just didn't. It was awkward and uncomfortable and different and weird.

Nothing like that has ever happened before. Even Mom doesn't touch or hold me like that. She probably never needed to touch me down there since I was a baby. Sometimes, Mom still calls me "baby" because I'm the youngest in the family, and even though I hate it, She's never done that before.

Worst of all, I hate how easy it was for John to know. He was fine with it! How? How was he fine with it?

I don't bother saying goodnight to J.R. or John like I usually do, even when Mom asks me to come out of my room to do that. I don't want to. I don't want to see or talk to them ever again. I don't care about practicing with John after school anymore. I don't care about dancing our routines at all. I just—I never want to see them again. Ever.

The front door opens and shuts and I think that means J.R. and John are gone. *Good*, I think. *I'm glad.* I don't want to see them again.

It's quiet in the house and I'm guessing it's because Chantel is at work and Michelle is out late with her friends. Even Alexis isn't crying. I don't know what she's doing or if Mom is taking care of her. I just run straight to my room when I get home and shut the door behind me and jump into bed and hide under the covers.

There's a knock on my door. *Knock knock knock.* "Roy," Mom's voice says on the other side. "Can you come out, please? What's wrong?"

"Leave me alone!" I shout with my face pressed into my pillow, holding tight to Charlie, my golden teddy.

Without saying anything else, I hear the doorknob twist and the door creak open. It happens slowly. Mom walks in, but I turn my back to her and keep it that way.

"Roy, baby," she says and sits down next to me. "What's wrong?"

"Fuck J.R.!" I say then.

"Roy!" she jumps. "Don't talk like that!"

"Why not?!" I roll over then. "J.R. said it! I hate him! I never want to see him again! Him or John! Fuck both of them!"

"What exactly did he do, baby?" she asks. I can tell she's upset, but I don't see why. She has nothing to be upset about. She doesn't know what he did, and I don't want to tell her! Nothing! Not a word. I don't. Let her figure it out on her own. I don't care! I turn back around and ignore her; pretend she isn't there. I don't want to talk to her. I don't want to talk about him. I just want to forget it ever happened. I want to forget everything about what he felt like, where his hand touched my skin, I don't want to remember any of it.

"I hate you! You're not my Mama! Your name's Victoria and you're not my Mama! I hate you! I want Daddy!" I shout at her again, my voice shaky, and I hate it. "Just go away, Victoria."

She doesn't say anything after that, just rubs my shoulder gently, and I hate that it reminds me of *him*. I pull away from her and her hand drops away. Then, she gets up and leaves. I feel her weight leave the side of my bed, and it doesn't feel like I'm slipping off to the side anymore. She leaves my room, says goodnight, and closes the door behind her. I don't say anything. I don't even move.

I don't know how much time passed, but I probably spent the next hour or more stuck remembering the details of what happened. The way J.R. looked, what he said and did, the way he smelled. I remember all of it and I hate all of it. The way he told me not to be shy when I said I wasn't shy, but he just kept telling me that anyway. The way he slid his hand over my shirt then under my shirt then under the waistband of my pants. I hate the way he touched me there and the way his skin felt up against mine. I asked him to stop and leave me alone, but he didn't, all he did was ask me why. I had nothing to tell him, nothing to say because I didn't want to be rude. So, he kept going. I remember the way his gruff voice started whispering while he touched me, not like anyone else I've ever heard whisper. It was like he was hiding something, but enjoying something—enjoying it. I hated it.

I shut my eyes to block it out. I didn't even notice the way my teeth clicked together or the way my jaw and fists tightened. I tried to forget everything J.R. did today, but he's just there, at the front of my head. His face. His voice. His touch. I see him, hear him, feel him, hate him. I remember John too, can't get either of them out of my head, no matter how hard I try. I try! I really do try, but it doesn't work. J.R. is just there. He and John are just there in my head and they won't leave me alone. They're there.

Chapter 4:
Repercussions

> "*Every human walks around with a certain kind of sadness. They may not wear it on their sleeves, but it's there if you look deep.*"
>
> —Taraji P. Henson

Roy hasn't said much of anything since he came back from John's place. It's been three days, and it's Saturday now. Most of the time, he's been alone in his room and I don't know why. Mom keeps going in and out of it to give him food and sometimes cash. She must be giving him at least a hundred dollars, at the very least. I can hear her talking to him. It isn't common for Roy to respond, though, and even if he does, I can hardly hear what he says to her in reply.

Today, he's sitting on the other side of the couch from me watching television, one of his favorite shows that he liked to watch with John. As far as I've seen, he hasn't talked to him, asked him to stay over, or done any dance routines with him after that day. He's become so quiet lately, which is odd. It's like he's less of the happy little brother I've always seen. I barely even see him smile anymore.

Whenever J.R. comes over to have dinner with us or to visit Mom, Roy always runs off to his room or the bathroom or upstairs, anywhere farthest away where he can't see J.R. I've just pretended not to notice, but it was pretty clear something happened that day.

So, Mom asked me to sit with him today and make sure he's okay. I wasn't called into work today, so I had the whole day to spend with Alexis and study for my upcoming science test on Monday. Alexis is currently sleeping soundly in her crib in my room. I have the baby monitor on loud beside me, in case she wakes up and cries. I'll be able to hear her even if I pop into the kitchen or bathroom. My textbook and notes are laid out on my lap.

While Mom is out on a date with J.R.—that's what I'm calling it at least, even though she's never explicitly said so—Michelle is out with her own friends. Roy, Alexis, and I are home alone. It's pretty chill so far. Roy is loose, not really laughing or smiling at his show or keen on interacting with me. Cartoons are one of his favorite hobbies. That and listening to rap, watching rap, playing board games with me—and sometimes Michelle— and eating food, though that's changed too. There are some days where he eats a lot and is constantly going back to the kitchen to snack and other days where he doesn't eat anything at all. I think he's even lost a bit of weight, which worries me because he's already a really skinny kid.

"Are you hungry?" I ask him when a commercial runs, knowing he didn't have much today other than a granola bar when he woke up. It's just after 1 p.m. and he's still in his pajamas. So am I. It's nothing special. It's just one of those days. Cloudy and rainy, but that didn't stop Michelle or Mom and J.R. from going out. It's not stormy or anything outside, just a light drizzle, but it may as well be inside. The tension in Roy is fairly clear. "Do you want me to make you something?"

He shakes his head, choosing instead to focus on the TV. I get up, set my books aside for the time, and head to the kitchen to grab a snack for myself. I find a bag of salt and vinegar chips in the pantry and decide maybe he'll want to snack eventually. *He must be getting hungry at least,* I think, *even if he doesn't want to admit that for whatever reason.* I pour half the bag into a bowl and grab a crisp apple from the basket. Then, I go back to the large sofa.

I set the bowl of chips on the table in front of him. They are mainly for him. I don't need to eat them, even though I want to. I'd just feel better if I saw Roy eat *something*.

"I said I didn't want anything, Chantel," he complains and leans against the arm of his side of the couch.

"I thought you might want to snack while you watch your show," I lie. "That's always fun. You sure you don't want to do that? Even later?"

"I'm not hungry," Roy repeats.

I don't say anything in reply, just take a bite from my apple, crunch on it loudly but unintentionally. If I weren't so worried about him, I would probably let the moment be, but I am.

"You hardly ate anything today. Isn't your stomach grumbling?" I ask.

"Nope."

That's what catches me. It's the way he says that one-word response that tips me off. He's lying. I can hear it in his voice, which means that he is hungry. Then, why isn't he eating anything? Is he trying to starve himself?

I slide closer to him, shuffle myself over so I'm sitting on the cushion next to him, our shoulders barely touching. He hardly pays me any mind, except for subtly trying to edge away from me and put space between us, which I find odd. I put a hand on his shoulder to get his attention, and that's when he flinches. It's not a heavy flinch, but the reaction is enough to surprise me as much as the action did for him. I'm starting to doubt he's even paying attention to his show anymore.

"What's been going on with you the past few days?" I ask then, not bothering to settle back into my studies, just holding my apple to the side and taking little bites. "You've been acting weird since you came home from John's place on Wednesday."

Roy is quiet for an moment, refusing to say anything. I wait for him, wait and see if eventually, with enough awkward silence between us, he'll say something. It's quiet in the house, dead quiet, and I'm really hoping that he will say anything at this point. Anything at all. It doesn't have to be an answer to my question or why he's being so moody and irritable. I'd just feel comfortable if he said *something* to me. It could be the stupidest or craziest shit he's ever said, some really wacky thing that happened on Wednesday at J.R.'s house, I don't really care.

Then, he opens his mouth, but says the exact same thing.

"Fuck J.R.," he says again, exactly as I've always heard him say it in his room all alone or with Mom. That's been one of his constant phrases lately. Although, usually, he yells it.

It's not the language that's surprising to me. Roy listens to a lot of rap music, and most rap music has swearing in them. It's just that swearing isn't at all in Roy's nature. He's always been the happy, friendly kid that behaves politely in front of everyone. Even when he was mad in the past, he never really lashed out and screamed. Lately, that's been the case, but not before. Even in his rap performances, whenever a swear word came up in the lyrics, he censored himself with another word. Fudge, bear, cap, shat. Anything that rhymed with the verse or suited the style of rap. Now, though, it's like he doesn't care.

"Come on," I nudge him gently with my elbow. "You know you can tell me anything, right? We're brother and sister. We're basically best friends."

Roy still stays silent. He doesn't speak, just continues to lean against the end of the couch, just barely looking at the colorful television screen. It looks like he isn't even enjoying that now, his show running but whatever's that's occupying his head taking over his control.

"John used to be my best friend..." he says then, his voice quiet and nearly muted. The television speaks louder than he, and it isn't even at a loud volume.

"Why?" I ask, not judging, just casually with a level of curiosity in my tone. "What happened with you and him? Did you get into a fight?"

That actually gets a short laugh out of him. A scoff. "More than a fight," he says and turns away again, leaning on the side of the sofa with his left arm dangling over the edge. "I hate him."

"But you get along so well," I mention. "What could possibly make you hate him?"

Roy is silent again. This time, I can tell it isn't with a reluctance to talk. He's just thinking, I can see that in the way he doesn't pull away any sooner. He must know that he can walk off at any point. I bet he's already considered it plenty of times before I even started talking to him, but he just doesn't. He's still, completely still, thinking.

"I don't know…" he says eventually and phases out.

I wait for him to say anything more, but he simply doesn't. A minute passes, a commercial break arises, then another minute, more of his show, and another commercial break. I know I should be getting back to my studies. I don't feel nearly as prepared for this test as I'd like to be, but this, I think, takes priority. I mean, Roy is my brother. I hate to see him so down like this all the time. It isn't like him.

"Hey," I start again, trying to get his attention once more. "Whatever happened with you and John, I'm sure it's nothing. I'm sure you can still be friends with him. You have a long history after all. If you need a break from him then—"

"Just stop, Chantel!" he interrupts, and his volume surprises me. "Stop! I'm not talking to John ever again! I don't want to even see him! I don't want him or J.R. to move in with us. Fuck J.R. and fuck John."

I don't know what to say back to that, in reply to his anger. I'm not used to it. Sure, Roy has been angry before, but he was able to calm down with enough time or with a talk with one of us—usually Mom or me. However, this time, it just feels worse. He's beyond angry, pissed, and nothing can quite tame him again. I guess that's what scares me. I'm scared that Roy will never be that happy-go-lucky giddy kid that I've always known, the type to carry a smile wherever he goes. Whether rain or shine, it doesn't look like he'll go back to the old Roy, and that almost makes me cry.

"Do you ever get the feeling that Mom doesn't love you?" he asks then, interrupting the sounds of the television and surrounding silence. The question surprises me.

"Huh?" I wonder aloud. I have no idea where this is coming from.

"Mom," he repeats. "Do you ever think she doesn't love you?"

"I guess, sometimes," I answer, unsure of why this matters. "I'm sure we've all felt that way at some point. Me, Michelle, you, but that's not true. Mom's always cared for us, all of us, equally."

"How do you know?" he asks, seeking some sense of proof.

"Roy, Mom's the one that cooked for us all these years," I explain. "She's big on keeping the house clean, tidying up after us, *because* of us. She wants us to live in a clean and happy place. Do you honestly think she would do any of that if she didn't care about us?"

"Yeah," he says, and I'm stunned by the way he puts it. Like it's obvious. "I guess I do. She might love you and Michelle, but she doesn't love me."

"What really happened that day, Roy?" I press again, holding tight to his knee. "Please tell me. This doesn't sound like you."

"I don't want to talk about it," is all he says, as always.

"You've been saying that for the past few days," I respond. "Can't you tell me something? If not to anyone else, to me? I promise not to tell anyone else if you don't want me to, but I just want you to talk to me. I'm here for you."

"Just drop it, Chantel," Roy says and stands up from his huddled position on the couch. He turns his back to me and begins to walk away. Though as he does, he mutters, "J.R. is a fucking piece of shit, I'll tell you that much, Chantel. He's a sorry gay ass motherfucker and John is too!"

That's it. That's all I hear out of Roy. He stands up in one quick fluid motion, says those words, and stomps heavily up the stairs. I hear him slam his bedroom door shut seconds later. The TV continues to blare its sound, the colors moving left to right, right to left across the screen, holding no meaning to me but almost seeming to leave me dazed.

Roy's words sit heavily with me as I attempt to ponder what they mean in even the smallest regard. Perhaps there's some sort of clue that will let me piece together the full picture of what's really bugging him, maybe not a full picture, but a fuller one. His voice echoes in my ear, in the forefront of my mind, replaying the words over and over on an endless loop.

Drop it Chantel. J.R. Is a Fucking piece of shit. All of what he said is stuff he's said already. Nothing really makes any more sense. However, there are just a few words that hold more emphasis than the rest, like *piece of shit*. I wonder why he emphasized those words at all. Was it just anger? Did he pick and choose those specific words? The latter seems absurd to me.

I may not know everything based on what he just told me, but I can figure out one thing, something I was under the impression of for a long time. That's J.R. There's something off with him, and whatever it is, that's likely what's causing Roy's strange behavior.

I wonder if Mom knows about this. I wonder if she knows what's bothering her son or if Roy was right when he said she doesn't love him or care. I hope that isn't true, but I can't deny that sometimes Mom can come across as unloving by the way she screams at us over simple things, little things. It's the way she doesn't do much for us other than cook or clean. The number of times Michelle asked if she could take us to the amusement park or a seasonal festival, it's uncountable, and Mom never did. She may have gotten us presents for our birthdays or the festive seasons, however few of them she could afford, but what else? It's probably selfish of me to think such a thing, but for Roy's sake I feel like I have to. I don't want him to go unloved by another parent, too. I don't want that for either of us.

Alexis wakes up crying. I hear her voice as clear as day and I jump to my feet to quiet the baby monitor on the coffee table before hurrying upstairs. She is stirring in her crib, with her teddy. With both hands, I reach for her like I used to for Roy a long time ago. It feels like just a week ago that I was holding him like I am holding her, helping Mom with her third child when her hands were busy. Again, the thought comes to me. What if Mom only wanted my help with him because she didn't want to look after him herself? Alexis pouts and squirms in my arms, and when I give her a pacifier she only cries more, harder and louder. I walk back downstairs and into the kitchen with her to retrieve a cup of warm milk resting on the countertop and give it to her. She accepts it happily and drinks greedily, practically begging for more when her magenta-colored sippy cup is empty.

The events of Roy's pounding upstairs and latest responses ruminate in my mind as I get Alexis a second cup from the fridge, pre-ready for warm-up. While waiting for it to finish heating to just the right temperature, I make a mental note to myself to ask Mom when she comes home if she knows anything about what's wrong. After all, she's talked to Roy the most the past few days. She has to know the depths of what's going on with him, more than me. Let it be privately or with Roy present, but I'm going to ask her.

I'm going to ask her about J.R. — I don't care.

Chapter 5:
Truth or Lie

"**M**om, can I talk to you?" I ask later that evening when Michelle and Roy have already gone to bed. It's quiet in the house at this hour, 10:16 p.m.

"Can it wait?" she replies and lets out a lengthy yawn. "At least until tomorrow? I'm tired and I want to go to sleep, Chantel."

This is nothing new for Mom. Sometimes, she gets like this—reluctant to talk when I use *that* tone of voice, like she knows I'm going to speak of something serious. It's funny. I used to think only kids did that. I tend to dread the day Alexis grows up to delay, delay, delay whenever I need to "have a word with her," because it's probably going to happen.

"Please don't make excuses this time, Mom," I almost feel bad complaining to her while I rock Alexis in my arms on the couch. Back and forth, back and forth, slowly and gently. "Can't you come sit and talk for a bit? I want to ask you something."

Mom makes a low groan, but I can tell she's trying to silence it. With the dark of the night peering through the windows, it doesn't do her much good. I can hear almost anything at this time of night. She groans and mumbles under her breath inconceivable words jumbled together that I can't understand.

It's happened before, always when her meds were fading out. As a long-term schizophrenic, she often can't function appropriately without taking her daily medication. She tends to carry a lot of delusional beliefs, things that aren't true about other people, or even us, and she's flat most of the time. She doesn't really show a lot of emotion. I don't think I've ever seen her super joyful or cry before. She's just bland most of the time. Her psychiatrist prescribes her meds, and that seems to bring back a spark in her voice. I think at one point, the doctor also related it to a mood disorder too, like major depression or bipolar.

"What did you want to ask me?" Mom asks. I suppose looking at little Alexis in my arms would spike her thoughts toward her. I try to ignore it like I do, without judgment.

"I wanted to ask about Roy," I start. "Why is he acting so different all of a sudden?"

"It's complicated, Chantel," she replies automatically.

I'm surprised at how quickly she responds. It's almost like she practiced that answer, like she knew this was coming.

"I don't think you'd be interested in the details."

"Why wouldn't I be interested in the details?" I almost shout at her then but hold myself back. "He's my brother. If something's bothering him, I want to help, but he won't tell me anything. I was hoping you would, if you really cared that is."

That seems to take her aback. Mom's face turns to shock all of a sudden. "Why wouldn't I care about you?" she asks, surprised, and I think maybe a little hurt, but it's hard to tell with the little meds in her system. There is a part of me that regrets saying that, but I just couldn't stop myself.

"I don't know…" I say and drift before drawing her attention back to what I want, *need* to know. "Mom, I just need you to tell me."

"Tell you what?" she asks.

"Who's J.R.? What's his real name? What do his initials stand for? Where does J.R. get his money from if he doesn't have a job? Why does he drive a car without any plates? Do you even know any of that?" I continue. "Ever since you paired up with him, you haven't mentioned who he is or why you even like him. He hasn't even said anything of himself. It's like his whole identity and his past is still a secret to us, and you don't even care. Ever since I first saw him, I had the sense that there was something off about him, I just didn't know what it was. Now, after Roy changed, I'm almost convinced that he had something to do with that day."

"What do you mean?"

"Mom, don't you see it? J.R. is probably the reason why Roy is so upset all the time and for how different he's been acting since that day," I explain. "I'm sure of it. I mean, Roy can barely be in the same room with J.R. anymore. He used to be able to tolerate him, but now, whenever he gets the chance, he runs off to his room or the bathroom or just a completely different place in the house. He won't even go near him."

She doesn't say anything after that, but I have to hope she understands where I'm coming from. I can tell by the way she doesn't meet my eyes that she knows something she's not telling me. They just stay down and refuse to come back up.

"J.R. is a complicated man," Mom only says in response. I can't believe it. "He's been through a lot in his life and doesn't deserve to be treated any less for what he has done."

"What exactly did he do?"

"That's none of your business, Chantel," she responds.

For a time, I can't speak. I'm just too shocked to hear that she would even tell me that. I know that isn't true. I heard her talking to J.R. as if nothing happened between him and Roy, but something must've happened, I know it. I just don't know what to say. I know whatever occurred between Roy and J.R. that day was bad, but for some reason she won't break up with him? It's like she's still desperate to see and speak to him. I still wish she would tell me. I wish she would be a little more specific and direct.

"What do you mean it's none of my business?" I ask. "We're a family! I think I have the right to know if something's bothering my brother. Did J.R. hurt him or something? Like—*abuse* him?"

"Oh, no," Mom counters almost immediately. "I'm sure it wasn't anything like that. Don't be so damn dramatic, Chantel. Roy was just shy and J.R. just helped him feel more comfortable. That's all."

"Since when is Roy ever shy?! That doesn't make any sense," I argue. "Whatever happened between them, it was probably a bad idea to let Roy leave with J.R. At least with Michelle's dad, Roy was safe, right?"

"There isn't much in life that makes sense, Chantel. That's just the way it goes," she says. "Do you think there was any reason for us growing up in poverty? Or any reason why Michelle has boys flirting with her already even if she chooses not to flirt back? Or any logic going toward you having Alexis at such a young age, younger than I was when I had you? Like I said, nothing much in this world makes sense. We just need to live with it and move on with our lives."

I don't understand why she is taking this so lightly, why she won't take care of her only son. I knew I sensed something weird with J.R., I just couldn't figure out what. I was stupid to think there was anything normal about him.

"How could you say that?!" I lash out because I can't hold back. "If something happened, it might be serious! We can't just ignore it! If he hurt Roy in any way, it could be considered an offense! J.R. can get arrested for that, and if anything like that did happen, he should!"

"Chantel, slow down," Mom says, stopping me. "This is why I didn't want to tell you. I knew you would overreact and take it wrong."

"How is that wrong?" I ask, but Mom only shakes her head in disappointment, as if it is embarrassing for her to hear me ask that. "J.R. is the one that did something wrong, I know it!"

"Chantel," Mom intervenes. "I still love him, okay? If you have a problem with him, then you can leave. This is my house after all, and I will talk to J.R. if I want to."

I don't know if I want to believe that. There's no doubt that Mom loves J.R. Whatever she sees in him, whatever he sees in her, I'm sure it started long before their first kiss. They probably fell in love when they started walking Roy and John to and from school together. Hell, they might've even caught feelings for each other before that. I have no reason to believe otherwise! The fact that I saw his interest in us so easily is enough to upset me more than I can possibly say. I should've seen this coming. I should've clued in that something could happen to me, Michelle, or Roy solely based on the wicked Valentine's Day gifts J.R. got for me every year. He didn't have to, but he did. That was strange enough to pick up on, and now, because I didn't act on that hunch when I should've, we have to deal with something that's probably worse. If not for me or Mom, then for Roy.

I just feel like it's my fault something happened to Roy because it's my responsibility to protect him. I'm the oldest. I *should* protect him. Now, Roy is angry all the time, and he won't stop lashing out or actively seeking trouble. He barely eats anything, he's lost so much weight, and it's only been a few days! He gets nightmares almost every night and wakes up screaming. I often hear Mom get up to go to his room and comfort him. On top of that, he keeps silently cursing at J.R., and at times, loudly as well. He asks for his dad all the time, more than he did before. He's changed so much in such a short amount of time. He's eight years old, and I regret not looking out for him like I should have with my suspicions.

"I can't just leave it, Mom," I tell her. "This is serious. If something's bothering him, I want to know about it, just like I'd want to know if anything's the matter with Alexis. I don't know why you can't understand that."

"There's nothing *to* worry about, Chantel," she says. "I was handling it and now it's handled. Roy is just fine, he's happy, and J.R. won't step into this house again."

That's when it hits me. After all this time, I get it.

"You've been paying him," I say. "The bills you gave him every week as 'allowance.' It was to keep him quiet about whatever happened, so nothing bad would happen to J.R."

"Right," Mom admitted with a single nod to her head. "I'm asking you to put this behind us too. What happens in this house stays in this house. There's no reason to cling to the past when the past is settled and done with."

"Are you serious?!" I question. "You can't make him be silent, Mom. It's not right and it's not fair. Roy shouldn't have to deal with whatever he has to deal with, not alone, especially at such a young age. If he wants to speak up, then he should. You can't silence me like him."

"Chantel, I'm not trying to silence you. I just don't want you to do something you'll regret in the future. Besides, Roy is fine with it. Why can't you be too?"

I don't believe anything Mom is saying. Roy is fine with it? Really? He's okay with getting money to stay quiet about whatever happened that day? He would rather do that than speak out? Speak to me or Mom or Michelle? Not only do I not understand, but if that's what he really wants, shouldn't I respect it? I don't know. I don't know if there's something more to this situation; it just doesn't make any sense to me.

I guess Mom is right. Maybe I should leave it as it is.

"Let it be, for Roy, Chantel," she tells me. "It's what he wants. So let it be. Don't bring this shit up anymore."

So, despite how much my gut is telling me not to, despite how much I want to open up and confront Roy and ask the question directly to him, I let it be. I let it go.

I take Alexis and storm off to my room, put her to sleep, and then attempt to catch some z's myself, but I can't. That same pressing question still lingers at the front of my mind. *What happened to Roy?* I roll over onto my side, from my left, then my right, then onto my back, trying to find a comfortable position to sleep and forget about it, let it be like Mom told me, but I just can't. I need to know.

So, I get up from bed and, in my pajamas and slippers, quietly make my way to Michelle's room down the hall. I knock on her door, once, twice, though I'm not surprised that she doesn't answer. She's probably just asleep. Michelle has always been a heavier sleeper than me. So, I walk into her room anyway and she's asleep. Spread across her single rosy pink bed, a leg dangling free from her blankets off the edge. She's turned over so her back is facing me with her nose to the wide window. It's dark in her room like it is everywhere else in the house, but at 3:14 in the morning, Michelle has the moon shining through her windowpanes. It gives me plenty of light to see her basic silhouette.

I walk forward slowly and quietly, sit on the edge of her bed, and shake her awake. Then, I whisper into her ear, "Michelle? Michelle, wake up."

She groans at me and turns. She knows it's me but doesn't want any part, any interaction whatsoever. "Go away, Chantel," she complains, her voice hoarse. "Go back to bed." She doesn't bother to open her eyes the smallest fraction to look at me.

"I need to ask you something," I tell her. "It's important. It's about Roy. Do you know what's going on with him?"

"Why would I know?" she moans at me, her sound rumbly through the night. "If something's wrong with him, he can talk to me himself." That surprises me but only for a moment.

I can't believe she wouldn't care about her brother like I do. Maybe I am just overreacting. Maybe Mom was right and I am taking this a bit too seriously. I mean, I don't even know for sure if J.R. had anything to do with Roy on Wednesday. That's my own brain making accusations but, for some reason, it just makes sense to me. Like, I can't see why he wouldn't have anything to do with Roy. The thought alone is enough to make it seem worse, at least in my head. So I have to know.

"Michelle, please," I continue. "Do you know if J.R. did anything to him?"

"What the hell, Chantel?" she replies in a low drag. "No, I don't, now just leave me alone." She pulls the blanket over her head, pretends I'm not there, and eventually starts gently kicking me off the edge of the bed. She's cranky and tired. She doesn't want to talk.

She doesn't know anything and she doesn't plan on knowing anything. She has no desire to ask Roy about it or even convince him to share. Mom probably told her to let it be just the same as she told me, and that's exactly what she did. Michelle doesn't want any part, be it at three in the morning or midday.

So, I retreat to my room and crawl back into bed. I shut the lamp off beside me and pull the covers over my body. For a while, all I do is stare up at the ceiling and think. I think about Roy, about what could possibly be bothering him and why he hates John and J.R. so aggressively now. I come up empty, and sooner or later I drift off to sleep.

In the morning, I find myself in a state of perpetual exhaustion. I wished I could fall back asleep again, but the rumination of Roy and J.R. and the mystery between them would not let me succumb to it.

There's just some kind of primal instinct inside me, or discomfort, or whatever whenever I think about J.R. and my little brother, and I can't stop asking myself:

Should I have done more? Should I have continued to press Mom for the truth? Do I let the matter die and not go back to it again? Do I let J.R. be as he is? Do I question him about that day? What would happen if I didn't decide to press for answers to find the truth with Roy or J.R. or Mom? Is it right to go back to Roy and ask again, dig deeper, try to get him to tell me anything more?

I'd feel a lot more comfortable if Roy told me what really went wrong himself or if he didn't want me to worry, that he wants the matter to be left alone. Only then do I think I could ever put it down and let it slide. Since he's never told me anything of the sort, that's all I can think of. Questions, questions, and just more questions.

I have no problems with Travis anymore or worrying about Alexis growing up without a dad. I can cross that bridge when or if I get there. My pressing concern is Roy. He's so young and doesn't deserve to be silenced from whatever unfortunate circumstances that J.R. seemingly put on him. Roy and Michelle and Alexis and Mom are really all that matter to me. Forever and always. So, I need to figure this out.

I just need to. Somehow.

Chapter 6:
Nieces and Nephew

*** *15 Years Later; September 2011* ***

"Hi there, how can I help you?" asks the lady at the front desk of the local beauty salon about a quarter of a mile from my apartment. It's called the *Mocha Goddess Salon*, and it's a place that specializes in eyelashes and hair extensions. The receptionist, who is also one of the stylists, greets me with a wide smile and her skin seems to glow under the bright fluorescent light, her hair a flawless turquoise.

"I have an appointment at 3:30 with Paris," I tell her. "Name's Chantel."

"Of course," she says, and I read the nametag calling her Sophie. I've been coming to this beauty salon for the past few years. Mom introduced it to me. "Come on in."

She leads me to Paris' workstation. It is bright inside the small salon. On busy days, it can be a little bit crowded, but today is not one of those. It's a Tuesday, and thankfully, I wasn't called in to work today. My supervisor at the insurance company I work for said I didn't need to be there. There are only a few other ladies getting their hair styled nearby.

Sophie leads me to a booth on the far right, around and behind the main reception desk, and has me seated in the black velvet chair. The large mirror stares at me and I stare at it. On the little ledge in front of the mirror are an assortment of combs, scissors, brushes, irons, and a hair dryer.

"What are you looking to get done?" Sophie asks while I settle in and make myself comfortable. This practice is nothing new.

"Just the usual sew-in for me please," I tell her. "And maybe a light style, some curls. We'll see."

Sophie smiles at me in the mirror. She is directly behind me, her hands on my shoulders. She covers me with a thick, black, water-resistant cover to keep me free of hair during my visit, then says, "I'll go get Paris and tell her what you're in for. Hang tight."

I give her a single nod and a gentle smile and she gives me a light tap to the side of my blanketed shoulder before scurrying off. I wait in the chair, gazing around, and at times watching through the mirror just an arm's length ahead of me. Usually, I get some color added too, but today I'm perfectly fine with brown and the casual silky sew-in.

By the time Paris comes over, she greets me with a large smile shining on her radiant brown face. She's got gorgeous blonde hair with highlights on the side. I've known her for a few years mostly because of Roy. We're pretty close, we keep in touch often, and are great friends. Paris is Roy's ex-girlfriend and the mother of Chad, Ashley, and Ariel, my nieces and nephew. They aren't together anymore. I guess things just never worked out with Roy's attitude and all. Ever since he started hanging out with the older boys at school and smoking weed, it's been downhill from there.

"So just a sew-in and your usual style today, Chantel?" Paris asks.

"That's the plan," I reply.

"How long would you like it?"

"About 16 inches or so," I say. Currently, my hair goes down past my shoulders and nearly halfway down my back. I always choose to get my hair sewn in whenever I come in to see Paris, and 16 inches always feel appropriate. I show her how long I'd like it to be too, using a hand to measure where I want it to end.

"Sounds like a good idea," she says, and begins to go to work.

She brushes through it, once with a standard hair brush, then again with a comb. Then, she leads me over to the basin where I can get it washed and conditioned before the design of the sew and style. I adore this part of hair salons mostly. The sensation of a soapy and fruity smelling shampoo is enough to soothe me completely. Sometimes, I'll even close my eyes to enjoy it fully.

"So, how's Alexis doing?" she asks as she's applying the conditioner. I know Paris' routine without even turning around, just the same as I know her daughter and she knows mine. They often play and hang out together since they go to the same school.

"Oh, she's great," I respond. "She moved in with me six years ago."

"So, you finally got your own place, huh?"

"Yup!" I admit. I'm proud of the thought. "Finally, I'm making enough income to support her and have my own apartment. I couldn't be happier for that."

"Tired of Roy and Michelle?" she asks, and in the mirror, I can see she's smirking, on the fringe of a laugh.

That makes me laugh, a light casual chuckle, but I return to seriousness when the memory of Roy's behavior unfolds. "No, not at all. Just glad to finally be out of the house and give Alexis her own home. I still miss the others though."

"Yeah," Paris says in an understanding tone while moving from my left to my right. "How's Roy doing?"

Paris is also aware of Roy's mental condition. I don't know if she knows exactly what happened. I'm guessing that was part of the reason why their relationship never worked out, a lack of communication. I don't recall Roy ever being enthused when it came to being open and honest with her, or anyone really, about what happened to him all that time ago.

"Doing better, I think," I reply, albeit with hesitation. "I don't really know, honestly. He lives with his dad most of the time. Has since you left, I'm pretty sure."

"Really?" she says. She sounds surprised. "What about the kids?"

In the time that Paris and Roy were together, they did manage to bring up three kids successfully without parting ways. The first to come was Ashley, a thin and delicate girl with dark skin who keeps her jet-black hair perfectly straight and aligned with her spine. She's six and probably the most confident of her siblings. I think she gets it from Paris. She takes great pride in her appearance even for a child under ten.

A year later came Ariel, who's five years old at this point. She's smaller than Ashley with a thinner frame and, in my opinion, she appears softer and more flexible, though she would never agree or admit that in front of anybody. I think she likes to be seen as the tough middle one. She kind of reminds me of Michelle.

Finally, the last to join them was Chad, a small chubby kid with short meticulous curly brown hair and high cheekbones. He's a year younger than the girls and is more shy and reserved from what I've seen. He's definitely one of the types to stay inside and play video games all day, I think. Hell, he's probably doing that now. He always is whenever I come to visit. You can tell by the way he's either in his bedroom in Mom's house or the home basement guiding a character of sorts on the flat screen.

"They're living at home with my mom," I tell Paris as she focuses on the final touches of the sew. "She runs a home daycare. I don't think Roy was ever too keen on looking after his kids like I am, probably thanks to J.R."

"Oh really?!" Paris notes. "When did that start?"

"A few years ago?" I estimate. "It's probably been about four or five now, but enough about my family. How's Danielle doing?"

"Just fine," she replies, "and transitioning nicely into pre kindergarten."

Danielle, Paris' third girl and little sister to Ashley, Ariel, and Chad, is a sweet girl. Alexis gets along with her, just as I do with Paris. Sometimes, she even babysits for her whenever I can't and when Paris is busy. She's got thick sandy brown hair, and I'd wager she'll be a heartbreaker by the time she gets into high school. She's smart and confident and even a little reckless for her age, but otherwise a cute little girl.

"How is everything going with her dad?" I ask.

Unlike my family or me and Alexis, Paris and Danielle have had a relationship with Mark, father and spouse to Paris. Danielle knows her father, and Paris gets along well with him.

"Oh, well, about that," she starts in answer. "We broke up."

"Really?!" I say, stunned at hearing her say so but trying not to move so Paris can complete the look on my hair. "I'm so sorry it didn't work out. You two seemed like such a great pair."

"Yeah, that's what I thought too, but things changed," she says with a gentle shrug without interfering with the way she holds the curling iron to style the rest of my hair into smooth alluring curls. Paris and I, we've known each other for years because of Roy, but we haven't spoken for months in person. No particular reason. We've just been super busy with our own schedules. It's been difficult to set up a date for coffee. Still, I am amazed at how easily she is taking it.

"How long?" I start to ask. "How long has it been?"

"Almost a year," she answers.

"And you aren't at all upset or heartbroken about it?"

"Well, obviously I am, Chantel," she seems to joke, however loosely. "But with this time I've had to myself, alone with Danielle, I've come to realize how much better off I am. I'm much happier than when I left, and Danielle seems to be handling it just fine. Sure, it was difficult to get back on my own two feet once he was gone, but I'm growing on them. It's getting easier." She studies me for a moment in the mirror. She can see me watching her closely. I know she means every word. She wouldn't joke about this sort of thing. I'm happy for her, I really am. "It'll get easier for you too, Chantel," she adds. "You'll see."

"It's not that, not really," I tell her, and she continues doing the rest of my curls. "It's just that I've been thinking about what's next. Sometimes I'm still not sure which way is forward with finding someone else, but at the same time, I feel like I'm wasting too much time."

"When it's right, it's right," she says with a basic shrug. "I'm sure you'll run into someone soon."

All I do is smile at her in the mirror, the grin wide on my face, and watch her curl the last little bit of my hair. It's looking good so far, better than good. It's looking fantastic.

"Enough about me," I say again. "What about you? I know it might be too soon, but do you plan on finding someone else?"

She sets her curling iron down on the ledge in front of me, unplugs it, and lets it cool off. "Maybe one day," is all she says. "But not today. It's going pretty good so far and I like where my life is headed."

Paris has always been a pleasure to chat with, whether at the salon or not. She's positive and enthusiastic and gives off such good vibes all the time. I appreciate her perspectives on life and topics like this. She's unlike anyone I know. After today, it's nice to be reminded of the fact that I can just take it slow. I don't need to move as fast as everyone else seems to be moving. Her words sit with me heavily at the front of my mind, *when it's right, it's right*. It's a nice thought, but I still worry.

Mom had to go through three breakups while she had me, Michelle, and Roy. Fifteen years ago, I experienced my first. I don't want to welcome a second or third just like her. I don't want to have to deal with that and I don't want Alexis to either. I'd prefer if I just take it slow, get to know someone, slowly and easily, and maybe Alexis can get to know them too and grow to like them just like me. I don't want to end up falling for some other man while Alexis hates that other man. No, I'd rather wait and see what happens. Just like Paris said, *when it's right, it's right*.

In the mirror, she smiles at me and unclips the cover from the back of my neck, and at last, I feel the open air reach my skin again.

"You're all done," she says. "How does it look?"

"Great!" I note with glee. "Thank you, Paris! It looks fantastic!"

So, the two of us head back to the front of the beauty salon and I pay the bill. It is $150 in total, and just as I'm returning my wallet to my purse and about to head out with a final gracious nod, Paris stops me one last time.

"Before you go, I thought I would let you know," she starts again, her tone gone serious and low. I can't even think to reply and ask what's wrong, only stare at her and wait for her to continue. "Danielle told me yesterday."

"Told you what?"

"Ashley, your niece and my oldest daughter," she says in a quiet voice and I have to wonder why her expression or voice has changed or what she is about to say. "I saw her touch Danny, very inappropriately I'll admit. I don't know where she learned it or why she would do such a thing, but she did."

"What?" I ask, shocked to hear this news.

"I don't know," she says, raising her hands beside her head as if there's a possibility that she's wrong and merely seeing it incorrectly. I can tell that she and I both know that isn't the case though. "Danny told me, and she was really uncomfortable when I talked to her about it after work. I thought you might want to talk to Ashley about it personally. Ask her why she thinks it's acceptable to be touching people like that. See her side of the story or whatever."

"For sure," I agree. "Thanks for telling me. Alexis and I are going to see them this weekend. I'll chat with her about it then and see what happened."

"Thanks, Chantel," she says. "I have a feeling it has something to do with what happened to Roy when he was a kid, but I'm not entirely sure."

"Don't worry, I'll figure it out."

Chapter 7:
Generational Curse

> "A lesson will keep repeating itself until it's learned. Life first will send the lesson to you in the size of a pebble; if you ignore the pebble, then life will send you a brick; if you ignore the brick, life will send you a brick wall; if you ignore the brick wall, life will send you a demolition truck."
>
> —Oprah Winfrey

When Alexis and I arrived at Mom's old place Friday night, the sun had barely begun to set. It is just before 7 p.m., 6:48 specifically. Mom and J.R. are the first to greet us when we get to the house.

It isn't all the time that we visit. I tend to avoid coming home to keep Alexis away from J.R. He is the one that touched Roy, after all. More than that – he molested him, abused him, touched him in a way he didn't want to be touched. I found that out myself, and I'm not letting anything of that sort happen to Alexis. The only reason why we show up once a month is because I'd like Alexis to get along with her cousins. I'd feel guilty otherwise, and sometimes I still do, for not letting them see each other more often.

Mom's house is exactly as I remember it. The garden is still beautiful and flawless. The flowers are open and vibrant and the grass is cut perfectly, evenly, orderly. Mom and J.R. wave to us from the front porch. Alexis and I grab our bags from the trunk of our white car and we head in.

"Nice to see you again, Chantel," J.R. greets when we step inside and remove our shoes at the door. Alexis immediately hugs him, and I can't deny, seeing that makes me bristle. "And darling Alexis. How have you two been since the last time we've seen you?"

"Just fine," I answer, trying my hardest to mask the coldness in my voice with calm. "And don't call her that."

I really didn't mean to sound rude. I just can't stand the thought that him and Mom are still together after all these years, living together now, as if it couldn't be any worse. I don't blame Roy for leaving and going back to his dad. Though I do feel bad for his kids, I'm almost proud of him in a way. With J.R. here, it's probably a smart decision to live at home with his dad.

J.R. moved in with Mom seven years ago in 2003, not long after Michelle, Roy, and I moved out. It's been mostly the two of them living at home running a home daycare together. I hate the thought of J.R. touching anybody else's kids like he did to Roy. It's disgusting.

"Alexis!" shouts Ariel, Roy's middle child, who comes running as soon as I shut the door behind me. Alexis moves past J.R. and she and her cousin embrace. They are ten years apart, but they get along well. "You're here!"

It isn't long before we're greeted by Ashley, the oldest among the three, though she and her sister nearly came out to be twins. They are only months apart in age. I'm glad to see them both, but within seconds, my nervousness seemed to peak, my mind spiraling with the thought of the kind of conversation I'm going to need to have with her thanks to Paris' comment.

"Girls," I acknowledge with a gentle smile and nod regardless. "Where's your brother?"

"Chad is in his room playing video games, Auntie C.," replies Ariel. She has always been the kinder one of the three, the "goody-two-shoes" if you want to call her that. "You can call him if you like. He might come."

"That's okay," I tell them. "I'll see him later at dinner. Why don't you girls go have fun before washing up to eat? We still have time."

So, they do. They run off toward their rooms. Ashley and Ariel are in the same rooms that Michelle and I once occupied and Chad is in Roy's previous room. I must admit, the interior looks different than the last time we visited. I forgot how well Mom kept the place tidy and how good her cooking smells. The smell of baked chicken and steamed rice and veggies wafts through the whole house.

With dinner nearly ready, Mom, J.R., and I have a seat in the living room. They sit side by side on the old gray sofa. It looks faded and torn in places too, aged with the years that Alexis and I have been away. I take a seat on the loveseat that appears just as faded. Then, we get to talking like we usually do every weekend.

Mom asks me how things have been going at work, with Alexis, if she's adapting well in school, if she knows what she wants to be when she's older, if she has a boyfriend. I tell her everything is fine with her and work is going well, that it's stressful in the insurance company month after month, but that I'm making enough to sustain the both of us. She smiles, but doesn't comment. I know she is waiting for the details.

At last, I sigh and tell her no, Alexis doesn't know what she wants to do yet and she doesn't have a boyfriend. It's not that I'm disappointed at the facts. It's just that I'm disappointed at the need to tell her. I don't think I should, but also, I get it. She wants to catch up and see where everything is going with us.

"That reminds me," J.R. interrupts while I tell them about Alexis copying my style of fashion and borrowing some of my clothes, though she doesn't return them, just keeps them in her closet. We're the same size in almost everything we wear. "Your hair looks good, Chantel. Did you get it done recently?"

The sudden compliment takes me aback and makes me grit my teeth. Usually, it wouldn't. I tend to enjoy them, but hearing that come from J.R., knowing about what he did to my brother, it makes me feel uncomfortable and I have to ball my hands into fists to keep myself under control. I always hate when the thought comes to mind of Mom keeping him around. Nonetheless, I respond because I don't want to be rude, "Yeah, I did."

I managed to keep my sew-in in my hair almost as well as Paris did it on Tuesday, and I'm proud of the way it looks. The same goes for the hair extensions that I absolutely adore. The one thing that looks different from that day is probably the curls. I tried to make them last as long as I could, but ultimately, I had to redo them. Still, they don't look as good as the curls that Paris put in my hair, but J.R. says it looks good on me regardless. He calls me Hollywood, the nickname he gave me since

I was in high school. I thank him but wish he doesn't notice. I always hated that nickname, especially from him.

"So anyway," I lead away then, steering the conversation to the matter that hasn't left my mind. "Mom, I wanted to talk to you about Ash."

"What about Ash?"

"When I went to get my hair done the other day, Paris told me that Ashley touched her daughter. You remember Danielle, right? Has anything of that sort happened here while I was gone?"

Mom is quiet for a moment, her expression bland. I can't tell if it's the effect of a flat schizophrenic or if she's just wondering what to say back to that. I suppose Mom has always been difficult to read.

"Not that I know of, Chantel. Why?" she answers finally.

"Why?! Because Mom. This is serious," I tell her. "It was embarrassing to find out that my niece touched someone else's kid. It isn't right and Paris said Danielle was really uncomfortable when they talked about it together. Has Ashley ever done anything like that before?"

"No," she says, and somehow I can tell that she's lying. That was far too quick of a response and was way too planned. She was all too ready to give me that. She has to be lying, has to be. It wouldn't be the first time.

"Are you sure nothing happened?" I ask her again. I really don't want to lash out or press with J.R. present. "You'd tell me if anything happened, right? I don't want to have to ask Ashley personally or think Paris was lying to me."

"Well, there was one...incident...we had a couple of weeks ago, but I don't think it has anything to do with Danielle." Mom admits, and at that I'm surprised.

"One incident? What incident?"

"Ash and Chad were just having fun in the basement, playing, whatever it is they do while Ariel was out with J.R.," she explains. "I checked in with them because they were being awfully quiet for a while, and I just found their clothes piled aside and Ashley over Chad. It seemed she, or they, were, I don't know, touching each other."

I'm speechless for a time, unsure of what to say or how to even react. I don't even notice the gaping hole my jaw creates until the air turns awkward and Mom asks me to say something. So finally, I do.

"What—" I start, still too shocked to move. I can't believe Mom isn't as concerned about this as I am. "And you—you didn't do anything about it? Not even ask her what she was doing?"

"Of course I asked her, Chantel," she says blandly. "I just figured they were having fun…in some sort of weird unorthodox way."

"That doesn't matter!" I shout. "Whether they were 'having fun' or not, touching each other like you say, that's bad behavior!"

"Now, Chantel," J.R. interjects. "I think your mother is right. Sometimes it's good to let children explore who they are, especially in the family so it doesn't get public."

"I don't care how good you *think* it is," I counter, pissed and astounded at just hearing him of all people say something like that. "It's disgusting and it shouldn't be allowed, especially with children so young! They're under the age of five for crying out loud!"

Mom and J.R. look at one another, then back at me, as if I'm crazy to think any differently. I don't care! I learned my lesson from my brother. I'm not going to let that happen again to his kids. Even if Roy doesn't want any part in being a dad to them, I don't want this to repeat.

I shouldn't even be sitting across from *him*. I shouldn't even be anywhere in the same room as *him*!

They call me upset, which I don't deny. *No shit I'm upset,* I think, *why wouldn't I be?! Why wouldn't they care?!* They tell me to calm down, but I just can't. I don't understand why Mom or J.R. don't want to do anything to fix this. Does that mean J.R. has something to do with Ashley's behavior, too? Should I doubt that? I don't think I should. It almost seems obvious to me now. I don't think I have any reason to believe that he wouldn't get involved in my nieces' and nephew's lives just like he did with Roy.

"I think it's best to put Roy's kids in therapy," I openly state to both Mom and J.R. "At least Ashley. Maybe not Ariel or Chad, but Ashley most certainly. I don't want her touching any other kids, like Danielle, again or doing anything of that sort."

"Chantel, I really don't think that's necessary," Mom states. "If it really makes you uncomfortable, then I'll have a talk with her myself."

"Will you?" I ask, very clearly skeptical and my faith in her lacking. "Because if you don't, then I will. I'll look into some professional advice too."

"I'll handle it, Chantel," she says again. "If you really think it's such a big problem, which it isn't, then I'll handle it. Just give me a week."

I sigh. Part of me hopes that she will talk to Ashley about her behavior, explain to her the difference between good and bad touch, or even ask her *why* she touched Danielle, her little sister, and Chad. Another part of me just doesn't trust Mom. After seeing her want to let Roy's experience pass in the dark, I just don't want to risk that happening again. Maybe it's pointless to tell her this now. Maybe I should just go to a professional without bothering to tell her or J.R. — I don't know, the whole repeat situation just makes me feel conflicted.

"Does Michelle know about Ash's behavior?" I ask them.

"She does," J.R. admits. "Your mother called her and told her too."

"What does she think about it?"

"She agrees," Mom says, glancing at J.R. through the corners of her eyes ever so briefly before again focusing on me. "She said that it's probably nothing to worry about, just like I'm telling you now. I think you're just overreacting, Chantel. Right, J.R.?"

"Maybe just a tad," J.R. notes, pinching his index finger and thumb together with half an inch of space apart. "Though, I must admit, your intelligence is impeccable, Chantel. I'd probably be worried just like you are if I thought the situation was that extreme."

All I can do is scoff at that. "Cut it out, J.R. Your flirtatious compliments didn't work back then and they won't work now. Stop trying. I'm telling you both that it is serious and we can't let this slide. It's your fault we're in this mess to begin with, J.R. I really don't care what you decide to do or if you want to talk to Ashley and them, at all, but I'll take care of this. I'm not covering this up like you did with Roy. Not again, and that's a promise."

I don't bother with saying anything else, even though there is still plenty more that I'd like to get off my chest and just shove into their faces, I simply stand from my seat and head off to find Alexis and the kids. I'd rather spend the rest of the weekend with anyway. Without another word spoken between us, I'm gone, out of the room, out of sight, and out of mind.

Chapter 8:
Spiritual Advisor

The following day, I wake up bright and early in the guest bedroom. I eat a quick breakfast with Mom while the others are still sleeping, shower, then change and head out early to find an old friend. She said we could meet for coffee today.

So, while Alexis has fun with her cousins, I head out to the local café It is barely 9 a.m., and it's a light and cool start to the morning, partly cloudy, the temperature must be at least 60°F. The café isn't far, and it is certainly a pleasant walk. I could use it.

I find Jessica sitting at a table on the outside patio, sipping her usual mocha. It's her standard drink of choice, still to this day. I haven't talked to her a lot over the past years, not like I did during high school. It's not that either of us don't care anymore. We've just gotten so damn busy with our work-life schedules. Plus, with the whole ordeal with J.R. and Roy and his kids going on, it certainly doesn't help with finding the time to meet up with her like we used to. I just had to see her, even if only for a little while, about what Paris told me.

"Hey, Jess!" I say to her upon greeting, and she looks up from her cup to smile at me with deep hazel eyes. "How's it been going?"

"Not bad, Chantel, not bad at all," she replies, clearly happy to see me again and eager to chat and catch up. We hug when we get close and her touch feels just like it always does — warm, gentle, and alluring. "How have you been? It's been a while, hasn't it? Like a few months or so?"

"Seems that way," I say, my smile never leaving my lips. I sit across from her in the empty white seat after getting my own vanilla latte, my own beverage of choice, and we start chatting.

There are about a dozen people sitting outside with us with more inside, all of them talking, laughing, and drinking their own blends of coffee, tea, and biscuits. I recognize some of them as neighbors from Mom's house, both old and new, and they smile and nod at me when I catch their eyes. A slight note of kind acknowledgement without drawing too much attention.

Jess and I talk about where we've been lately and what we've been up to. I tell her how Alexis is doing, that she's in high school now and doing well, and that I'm working at an insurance company, though I don't tell her which one. I'm thinking of a career change sometime in the future, maybe not anytime soon, but part of me doesn't want to work there for much longer. It isn't that it's not fun or the people are trash, no. I just want a change. I want to do better for Alexis. I tell Jess too, and she tells me similar stories and events that have been going on in her life.

She goes into talking about her son, Drake, who's now just a few years younger than Alexis and is doing great. He's popular and smart, kind and caring, and Jess speaks proudly of him. She tells me about her anniversary trip with her husband, Jake, that she recently took while Drake was with his grandparents. She went to Europe for a month and she even shows me pictures of the trip. Scenery, architecture, and farmland in England, France, Italy, the Netherlands, Germany, Ireland, Sweden, and more. She did nothing but travel all month from the end of July to the end of August.

"Wow," I remark, certainly impressed and rather jealous. "These look amazing! I wish I could've been there with you."

"Aw, don't worry, Chantel," she says with a wave of her hand. "I'm sure at some point we'll be able to go together. I can even show you around next time!"

"True," I say and emit a short laugh before sipping again from my latte. The vanilla seems to hit me just right this early in the morning, giving me the sense of energy I need to work up the courage to ask what I'm meaning to ask. "Anyway, Jess, you still do readings for people, right?"

"Sure," she answers, taking a long swig from her mocha and seemingly not giving the question much thought. "Readings *of* people actually, but yeah."

Jess had been doing this ever since we started high school together. She's developed a niche for it. She's an empath, always has been and is now much more so. Whenever we walked to or from school together, with others or by ourselves, Jess has always been interested in reading strangers' expressions, emotions, body posture, sometimes even thoughts or drives or motivations. It's in her nature. Psychic readings have been a part of her family for generations, and she's always been good at it, at least to me.

"Yeah," she responds when I tell her how cool I think it is. "It's pretty awesome. You'd be surprised by how many people are into getting personal readings done for themselves. Of course, it doesn't surprise me, not since the beginning."

"Really? Why not?"

"People want to stay in the know," she explains, and I can tell she's close to nerding out just like she used to. The thought makes me smile. She feels like some sort of spiritual advisor again — not to say that she never was because in my mind, she always was. "They want to see if they're going to be successful: land that job interview, find the perfect lover, nail their desired career, be happy and have peace. They want to know what kind of challenges they'll face and if they'll overcome them. If something doesn't work, they want to find out why. We're mysterious creatures, Chantel," she tells me, "but our patterns can also be predictable."

I smile at her, completely mesmerized and stunned to see how much she's grown since the last time we'd spoken. It's obvious she's been learning a lot and that she's much better than she was before. I'm not complaining. I think it's amazing, but still, there's a small part inside of me that thinks it's hysterical.

"Sometimes, I think you get crazier every day," I state playfully, my smile unwavering and gleeful at her eagerness.

"Shut up," she kids and slouches back in her chair. "Why are you really asking about my psychic readings, Chantel? Do I need to read someone for you?"

"Yeah, if you're not too busy, I was wondering if you could do one for my nieces and nephew," I ask slowly and politely. "I hope that isn't too much to ask."

"Girl!" she shouts then. "Of course not! I'd be happy to! And for no charge as well."

So, once we finish our drinks, I walk with Jess back to Mom's house and we continue talking about our days. What they've been like lately, busy, busy, busy, and why. We even schedule a date to meet again soon.

I tell her why I'd like her to read my nieces and nephew. She says it's no big deal and explains the procedure. She's a clairvoyant, always has been, which means she has a gift for seeing and hearing what is really going on within a person. She uses extrasensory perception to understand others in ways I have never seen. Ever since we were in high school together, she always claimed that a spirit talks to her during her readings and sends her clear and vivid pictures on a person, and she says she just relays their messages. I don't know if I believe her, but it seems to be fairly similar to what she used to do when we were in school. I just don't remember there being so many details.

Jess and I enter my childhood home, and we're greeted by Mom and J.R. who are nestled together on the living room sofa watching an old movie. They hardly turn to us as we come in. Mom continues to watch the screen, while J.R. is the only one to open with a kind and bland, "Welcome back, Chantel!" His eyes never leave the television.

I wave an awkward hello and let out a small smile. I reply, "Hey J.R., are the kids around?"

"They're in the basement," he says. "Should be anyway. Playing their own games."

"Thanks," is all I reply, and lead Jess to the basement stairs. I offer her a glass of water before we go down. She politely refuses.

Sure enough, they are down there. At first I'm worried I'll find a pile of clothes like Mom said yesterday before dinner, but I'm quickly relieved to find them all dressed. It almost gives me a layer of hope. However, the fact that Jess doesn't say anything when we see them, despite her requesting silence, is enough to keep me alert and praying.

All four of them stop playing when they see us. Ashley, Ariel, and Alexis turn to watch us as if something is wrong. Even Chad pauses his video game. I look at Jess, wondering if it's okay to tell them to continue what they're doing. She nods at me.

"Girls, Chad, you remember Jess, don't you?" I ask, and they nod. Alexis even notes her as my high school bestie to jog Chad's memory. "She'll be staying over for a bit. Don't mind her. We just thought we'd drop by. Just ignore us."

Without being told twice, they do. Chad resumes his video game, holding the controller in his lap, the wide screen glaring its bright colors less than ten feet away from him. Ashley and Ariel continue playing at the dollhouse. Alexis mostly watches them, having grown out of dolls long ago. Though, occasionally, she pitches in to their game.

I stand side by side with Jess who studies them "like our English texts" in the twelfth grade. A picture that I would've thought to be somewhat creepy at first glance, turns out, isn't at all. Jess has her hands on her hips, watching closely to their postures, listening intently to their language. I don't even know the depths of what she's looking for.

It isn't until Ashley notices her staring that she stops and her sister does too. Chad does not, and Alexis is on her phone going through messages.

"Why are you both watching us then?" Ashley asks.

I look at Jess, she doesn't look at me. Her hands go down from her hips and one waves casually out in front of her. "Don't worry about it," she says gently. "It doesn't matter. You girls have fun."

Then she turns to me, leads me away and back upstairs. The entire reading, seemingly, takes up to ten minutes at most. She shows me outside to the backyard and we sit at the patio where we can talk privately.

"So," I start. "Did you pick up anything? You know how old they are?"

Jess nods, though it's clear that it's a serious nod, as if she picked up on something or heard an ancient spirit tell her something cruel. "Ashley and Ariel — close in age, my guess, is that they're separated by only a few months apart. Ariel, the middle child, acts much more mature for her age while Ashley is the smartest of the three. Chad is the youngest. How am I doing so far?"

I smile and reply, "As perfect as your readings always were," and wait for her to continue. I'm always amazed at how accurate she is with understanding other people's lives. It always seems like she knows them even if she doesn't.

"Yes, well, as for the question you asked earlier about whether or not they were molested, it turns out, I have picked up that energy from them. At least Ashley and Ariel. They seem to show signs of being touched by someone and carry more bodily urges and sexual feelings than other six year olds. You were right, Chantel."

"Who?" I ask, almost desperate to confirm or deny my suspicions. "Who touched them?"

"J.R.," she answers. "Your Mom's creepy boyfriend who's watching a movie with her. Does your Mom know anything about it?"

At that, I turn my head down and away from her. I look toward the chair, table, patio stones, grass, even trees. Anything but her eyes, somewhat embarrassed to consider the answer to that.

"I really have no idea," I tell her. "I know my Mom knows about J.R. touching Roy, and yesterday she told me she caught Ashley touching Chad the same way, but I don't really know if she knows J.R. is the cause of their behavior."

"Is she trying to hide it?" she asks.

"Probably," I say intuitively. "She tried to hide what happened to Roy all that time ago. Kept silencing him with money. I'm pretty sure she still does. Michelle is in on it."

"Why?"

"Honestly, I have no idea," I admit. "What about Alexis?"

"Oh, yes," she continues. "Her too. J.R. tried to touch her as well, but she isn't suffering the same results as the others. It seems like she was old enough to stop it and that's exactly what she did. She likely told him that if he did touch her, then she would tell someone, and he backed off."

There's a silence between us for the next few minutes, and we hear nothing but a soft breeze blow through our hair and the trees. I can tell Jess is watching me, probably seeing me think and process it all. In truth, I'm glad Alexis stopped it. I'm glad she wasn't affected, at least not like Roy or her cousins. It's still them that I'm worried about, and I have no doubt that Jess knows that.

"You've got to tell someone about this, Chantel," she says to me then. "If it happened to Roy, and now his kids, who knows what will happen next?"

"I know, I know, but who would I even tell?"

"Uh, the authorities?" Jess states, as if it's obvious. "Did you not pick up on it, Chantel?" I don't respond, just stare at her quietly and wonder what she's referring to. I wonder if she also picked up on the suspicions I had about J.R., now and even a long time ago, about his strange behavior. An awkward moment passes before she can see the confusion in my eyes. "I don't expect you to be psychic or anything to be able to see it, Chantel," she continues then. "Even with your suspicions, I thought it would be clear."

"Jess, what are you talking about?"

"J.R. is just an alias," she clarifies. "I don't think it's his real name or initials. It's likely he's done what he did before with other children, not just Roy. In fact, I'm almost certain of it. I think he only goes by it because he's a sex offender."

Chapter 9:

Open Clash

> "Every morning, we get the chance to be different. A chance to change. A chance to be better."
>
> —Alan Bonner

Now I know for sure what J.R. is, and after Jess confirmed it, I don't know why I didn't realize this before. I confront them about it just as their movie is rolling through the credits.

"Who are you, J.R.?!" I barge in, pissed and rattled. "Are you or are you not a sex offender?! I want to know right now!"

"Woah, well that's…bold of you to assume," is all he replies with initially.

"Chantel!" Mom chastises, but I hold up a hand to her in a gesture to drop it. All I really want to know is the truth as quickly and sincerely as possible. My eyes don't look at her once. They remain only on J.R.

"No, I don't care!" I say. "I want to know who he is, for real."

Jess still stands with me, rooted a few feet behind. She is quiet and attentive, watching as she usually does. I'm tempted to just get Alexis and storm home before this monster can even reply, but part of me really does want him to tell me even if the truth is unlikely to come out.

"In my years that I've known you and your family, never once did I take you as an accuser, Chantel," he says, and his tone does more than upset me. "All I saw was how intelligent and beautiful you and your siblings were."

"Come on, Chantel," Mom goes on, "What's with these accusations? Wherever you heard these rumors, I can guarantee that they aren't true."

"Can you?! Can you really?" I ask her then, at last turning to her. She looks plain, bland and plain. Her voice hardly sounds with anger or frustration. "I'm telling you, Mom, I have valid reasons to believe that he's not who he says he is, and if you think I'm wrong, why not tell him to give his real name so I can search him up on the registry? After all, if he's as innocent as he says he is, then he should have nothing to hide."

"Chantel—!"

"No, I'm serious, Mom," I continue, unafraid of backing down. "If you can't see him for who he really is, then Alexis and I aren't coming over again. I don't want her exposed to him, like Ashley, Ariel, and Chad. I suggest," I add, giving pause to sneak a breath or two in to make sure they're both paying attention, "that you have him leave and put those three in therapy. If you really care for them, at least."

I don't wait around to hear her reply, just let them sit with what I said, and I turn my back to run downstairs. Jess watches me, I can tell, as I go and grab Alexis in the basement. I tell her that it's time to go and ask her to get her things so we can leave. I really don't want to be in this house anymore, with that man that should not be named, while knowing how close he is to my nieces and nephew.

"Where are you going?" Ariel asks innocently.

"Are you leaving already?" Ashley questions too.

"We need to go," I tell the two of them, not giving Alexis a chance to answer herself or question why. "Come on, Lexie."

The girls don't make any more counter arguments, and Chad just continues playing his game on the widescreen television mounted to the wall, apparently not paying us much mind. So without another word between any of us, we head back upstairs. Once Alexis has her bag packed and her shoes tied, the three of us walk out. I offer to drive Jess back home and she nods and agrees.

In the car, I can tell she's a little shaken. She doesn't say anything until a respectable five minutes pass and we hit a red light. "That was intense," she says. "Are you okay?"

"Yeah, Mom," Alexis asks just the same, for once looking away from her phone. "What happened? Why are we leaving so soon? It's only Saturday."

"I'm fine," I assure both of them, then think better of it. "I'm just upset, that's all. I'd feel a lot more comfortable if we were home."

Alexis leans forward, puts a hand on the back of my headrest. "What happened?" she asks, persistent and confused.

I sigh. "It doesn't concern you, Lexie," I reply and strum my hands on the steering wheel, as if I'm impatient with the wait for the green light. I have no doubt that Jess understands how little of the action is impatience, and how it's really just nerves and rage acting as one instead. Regardless, she doesn't comment on it, and I continue in that same cold voice, "It's between your grandmother and her boyfriend, and we're not speaking to them again. We're going home. I'm dropping off Jess at her apartment and we're going home, Lexie."

That's exactly what we do. Not another word is exchanged between us. I focus on the road while Jess and Alexis seemingly watch the city scenery pass. Every so often, I catch Alexis glaring down at her phone, not paying the situation much more of her mind. I search her for signs, just like I might find in Ashley or Ariel or Chad, but I'm not as good as Jess is, so I don't find anything. Everything appears normal with her.

By the time I pull into Jess' apartment lot, she grabs her handbag and is on her way, into the lobby and upstairs. Before she's out of sight, she tells me to call if I ever want to talk or go for coffee again. I only nod at her in response. Then I resume to coast my car, a small white vehicle, out of the lot, onto the freeway, and back to our home. Alexis still refuses to say anything on the drive, and I have the feeling that she's mad at me because we're leaving before we're supposed to. I wish I could explain to her why, but I'm still trying to figure out how much to tell her, how much I *should* tell her. I still feel guilty about her dad being out of the picture. Even though I told her years ago that it was *his* decision to fraternize with other women, and Alexis made it clear to me that she wasn't mad, that she understood, I feel bad that he isn't part of her life. I don't want her to grow up without interaction from her cousins either, but I just don't know what else to do.

We get home when the clock on my phone reads 4:17 p.m. The small two-bedroom apartment is empty and maybe that's due to the present situation at hand. Alexis drags her backpack to her room, but before she shuts the door, I ask her to come to the kitchen table so we can talk. She nods, obliges. She's always been an obedient girl, mine, and I'm proud of her.

"Are you going to tell me why we aren't staying at Grandma's for the rest of the weekend?" she asks curiously. "What happened with Grandma and J.R.? I don't get it."

"I just wanted to get you out of that house," I tell her, taking a seat adjacent to her. "I wanted you away from J.R."

"Why?"

"Your cousins haven't told you?" I ask, only partially surprised. In truth, I don't expect them to tell her what he did. Alexis shakes her head, letting a minute pass in silence. I bite my lip, still wondering what to really say.

"J.R. isn't who he seems," I start. "He's a sick man with dark secrets, Lexie. I didn't want you to be a victim just like your uncle was or your cousins."

"A victim?" she questions, like this is all new to her. "A victim of what?"

Another sigh escapes me before I continue, "Do you know why your uncle isn't actively involved with his kids? With Ashley, Ariel, or Chad?" Again, Alexis shakes her head. So I explain, honestly and truthfully, as much as I can. "It was because when he was young, J.R. touched him. He was only eight at the time, and he didn't want to be abused. My mom—your grandmother—used to give Roy money to keep him quiet about it so J.R. wouldn't get into trouble. Your Auntie Michelle did the same thing when Grandma couldn't. I'm pretty sure they're both still giving it to him.

"Where is Uncle Roy?" she asks. "I hardly remember him since he left, which was probably when I was, like, five. Where'd he go?"

"He went to live with his dad," I answer. "He's still staying there today because he didn't want to be anywhere near my mom or J.R. I honestly can't blame him." I pause to see her reaction. She is only waiting for me to say more. "A long time ago, he asked that I drop everything about what happened to him. He didn't like that I tried to press him to tell me what really went wrong. I think he just wanted to forget. Now, I'm realizing that forgetting doesn't change anything. It gives mercy to the villain, which shouldn't be allowed. Because Roy chose to ignore what happened to him, that lets J.R. act again. Now Chad, Ariel, and Ashley are the ones that are suffering."

"They don't look like they're suffering, Mom," she disagrees. "Aren't you just overreacting? I mean, I get why Grandma doesn't want to speak out about it. If she really loves J.R., then she'd want to protect him. Ashley and Ariel seem fine. Maybe Chad is a little quiet compared to others, but I wouldn't think anything of it."

"She's protecting him for the wrong reason, Lexie," I state. "Because of that, I have to see my nephew in the same condition as my brother. I don't really care if Ashley and Ariel are okay with it. I hate to see this become a repeating tragedy in our family." Alexis is silent then. She won't say anything and she won't look up at me for a long few minutes until I speak again. "I don't want you to be looped into this just like they are."

"Me?" she asks, and that same level of confusion is strikingly clear in her voice again. "What do you mean?"

"I just want to make sure, Lexie," I tell her. "Did J.R. ever touch you or flirt with you or anything of that nature?"

She is silent again, her head and chin tucked down. I can't tell if she's hiding something from me or just struggling to answer. Why would she struggle to answer? It's a simple yes or no, that's all I need.

"No..." she finally says, her voice almost mute.

"Lexie..." I warn only so subtly with an edge to my voice. "Don't lie to me. I want to know the truth. Did he?"

Alexis fiddled with her fingers. I can tell by the way her arms move gently but nervously and how her eyes won't meet mine. Soon, she brings them up to twirl her hair around her index.

"He hasn't really touched me ever," she says, and that brings some relief to me. "I think he tried."

"Tried?"

Alexis nods, says, "He technically did try I guess, but I didn't let him. I didn't want him to touch me, so I told him no, and that if he ever did, then I would tell."

I sigh then. I should've expected something like that to happen. I should've guessed that it'd happen to Lexie too.

"How long ago?" I ask her.

"Like, a few years ago?" she guesses. "Heck, I don't know, Mom. It happened a while ago. There's no need to worry, nothing happened. He didn't do anything."

"That's not the point, Lexie," I tell her, pinching the bridge of my nose. "Well, it is, but the bottom line is that he tried."

Alexis says nothing. All of a sudden, I hate J.R. more than ever before, or whoever he really is, and I hate Mom for keeping him around and letting this get so out of hand. This never should've happened to anyone in our family, and I feel like the cause of it happening at all—to Roy, to Chad, to Ashley and Ariel, and nearly even my daughter. Why wasn't I paying closer attention? Why didn't I do something about it earlier when he gave me a Valentine?

I sigh with hatred and anger. Anger at J.R. and Mom and me, but most of all, *me*. He's a fucking monster, and Mom might kept him around, but it's me that didn't do anything even though I saw how strange it was for an older man to go after the younger ones in our household. My suspicions should've tipped me off, as little of them as I had, and I hate that I thought it was nothing to worry about. Now what am I supposed to do? With J.R.? With Mom? With Roy and Chad and the girls? I'm not sure.

"Mom?" Alexis says, startling me into the present. "What are you going to do? Are we ever going to see Grandma again?"

I must've had that face again, I think, the face I usually have when I'm deep in thought about a serious situation. Alexis knows how serious this is to me. I hope she knows how serious this is to her as well. I don't want anything like this to happen ever again, not to our family, not to anyone.

"I don't think so," I reply to her then. "I prefer if we both stay away from J.R. and Grandma, at least for the time being. If things ever change, then I might consider going over to see her and your cousins again. For now, I want you to stay away from them. Do you understand?"

She nods, doesn't say anything in return. Just nods.

Chapter 10:
Shaken Up

     Alexis continues school, and I keep going to work. She's in the eleventh grade now I'm working for the second insurance company I've been hired at over the years. It is just as dull as the last but my position has grown up the ranks to administrative manager. Our days blend together just as they used to, following one after another, turning into week after week.

     Everything is normal, if it weren't for the constant back and forth talk about Mom and J.R. My phone rings for the third time today. I glance at it to find that the caller is Michelle. We've been talking a lot lately ever since I decided not to bring Alexis back to see her cousins. It's been a month. So, I pick it up and answer, heading out of my cubicle and into the break room to talk to her without distractions.

     "Hey, Michelle," I start on the way over there. It is not far—less than twenty steps away. The main offices of Nivea Health Care are wide open rooms consisting of bright lighting and at least 50 cubicle office spaces. Mine is situated close to the far right, five away from the break room, while my manager's office is on the other side behind a glass wall. "What's up?"

"Same old things," she replies on the other end.

"Right," I say. "Any news on exposing that bitch ass?"

"Yeah, uh, about that, Chantel," she says, her voice sounding small and delicate all of a sudden. I'm not used to it sounding like that. "Mom and I have been giving it thought, and I don't think it's the best idea."

At that, I'm confused. We've talked about J.R. for the past week or so. There've probably been dozens of phone calls of us talking about him, enabling us to find the best solution for his past behaviors. I don't want him touching any of my nieces or Chad or Alexis. Hell, I don't want to give him the opportunity to do that to any of the kids Mom is babysitting in her home daycare. That's way too big of a risk to take.

"What do you mean?" I ask her. "I thought we agreed to do something about it…"

"Yes, but just think about it," she says. "If you go to the authorities, confronting them about J.R., Mom could be in serious trouble. Just like how if we spoke about this through text, it won't look good on us nor would it look good on her."

"Look good?" I nearly exclaim. I can't believe it. "That's what you're worried about?! You're not at all concerned about the kids she's looking after? Ashley, or Ariel, or Chad?"

"I am," she says. "But you're missing the point, Chantel. It's not worth it if it means getting Mom into trouble."

"Who cares if she gets into trouble, Michelle!" I state then, keeping my shouting voice just low enough so my coworkers passing by don't overhear but at the same time with enough strength to deliver my message. "J.R. is the fucking pedophile. If Mom isn't going to leave him, then what choice do we have?"

"Have you ever considered *why* Mom doesn't want to leave him, Chantel?" she asks, but before giving too much pause to let me reply, she answers herself, "Probably because she *loves* him. Why can't you just let them be?"

"She loves a pedophile more than her own family!" I exclaim again, making sure no one else around me is listening. All of a sudden, I'm way too worried about that aspect when it comes to speaking about this in public. My voice grows just a little bit quieter. "I don't understand why you aren't taking this as seriously as I am. You should be taking my side." I pause, wondering if she will explain but knowing she won't. Michelle never took my side on stuff that's not even remotely related to this. She was the one that always tried to plot against me and get me and Roy into trouble. "What that man did to Roy, Chad, and both of our nieces, it's inhumane. It's an injustice and it shouldn't be allowed. I don't want this to be a common trauma in our family, Michelle, you need to understand that."

"I do—"

"No, I don't think you do," I tell her. "You just want to protect Mom for keeping that asshole around. Please, I'm practically begging you, don't be her pet. For once, see how many people, *children*, are involved that that man is hurting. Roy doesn't want anything to do with his kids, but that doesn't mean they should be neglected and unprotected. We need to stand up for them. They're only six years old! Chad's even younger!"

"Calm down, Chantel," she says as if it's no big deal. "Mom's been putting Chad in therapy for the past few weeks like you said. If you want, I'll even offer to put the other two in therapy too, the girls, and I'll pay for it myself. I just don't think any of this is worth going to the police about it. Mom is handling it just fine on her own."

"If that were true, she would've left that man a long time ago," I reply. "Like, Roy's time ago. She never would've kept that monster around."

"Chantel, I think you're missing the point," Michelle says again, an irritable groan at the back of her throat. I can tell she's trying her hardest not to let it go. "Just—try to put yourself in Mom's shoes. If you loved him—"

"I wouldn't love him."

"But if you did," she continues, "and you knew what he did to Roy, could you break apart your relationship with the man? I mean, you can't really blame her. Mom's been through three breakups. That's more than you've ever been through. She's obviously not going to want to go through another one, would you?"

"I can find another way," I tell her through gritted teeth. This whole situation is annoying me. Why can't Michelle just agree with me for once in her life? Why does she have to be protecting Mom after everything she's trying to cover up? More importantly, I hate that she had to bring Travis into this and loop my love life into the whole mess. I have nothing to do with this! This is all on Mom and that bastard, and I won't stand to watch our family be torn apart because of him. God forbid, if I did have feelings for him, then yes. I would find another way. "They could live apart from each other just like they used to, and those daycare kids and Roy's kids would be safe."

"Would they?" Michelle counters. I can't believe she's doubting me. "Come on, Chantel. You know that J.R. used to come over to Mom's place all the time when we were kids. Even when he didn't move in, he was there all the time. Do you really think that would've stopped him?"

I stare into the distance of the office space, above all the heads, over all the tops of the cubicle walls, straight and across to the other side. I'm not looking at anything in particular, just staring at an endless color-filled void, listening to every word Michelle is telling me in the receiver and trying to figure out who's side she's on.

"You sound like you're on my side…" I eventually say when she stops.

"I don't want to pick sides, Chantel," she responds. "I'm just looking at the facts. Love is a strong force. Nothing can stop Mom and J.R. from interacting together whether J.R. did those things to our family or not, and they'll probably do anything to keep seeing each other regardless of what we do."

"You're saying it's pointless to go to the authorities and report him?"

"I wouldn't say pointless," she denies. "What J.R. did is still shitty, I guess, but I just think it's unnecessary to press charges against him, unnecessary even to get Mom involved like that. Just think about it. If you do press charges on J.R., they'll not only question him but her and all the victims, including Roy and Chad, Ashley, and Ariel. Roy told you to drop it a long time ago, Chantel. Why can't you just respect that?"

"He hurt our brother, Michelle!" I shout then, hardly close to caring who hears me. "He molested him, abused him. Him and his kids! I don't understand why this doesn't upset you as much as it upsets me! It's an offense!"

"Can you really blame me though?!" she shouts back in return. I can tell by the way her voice shakes that she's close to crying on the other end. At this point, I don't really care. "Mom has been through a lot, both before and after she met J.R. He helped her. I don't want to see Mom hurt because of this, Chantel. You should understand why she doesn't want to leave him."

"Leaving someone doesn't mean you can't find someone better," I tell her, an edge to my voice. "Besides, if Mom really cared about any of us, she wouldn't let that monster stay, period. Now, are you going to help me with this or not?"

I'm done with this entire conversation. I can hear Michelle sniffle on the other end. I know she's crying and I really wish she wouldn't. I don't want to talk about this anymore, I don't want to hear her tell me I'm completely in the wrong because I know I'm not.

A brief moment of silence passes between us, though it feels just more awkward when all I can hear is her breathing. It is heavy. Then she sighs.

"No, I don't want to help you press charges against him, Chantel." I could swear my jaw gapes at hearing her say that. She's just—

"You're giving up?"

"No," she says almost immediately when I ask. "It's just that, I've been studying this stuff in school, not the events that take place with a man like J.R. specifically, but about the effects this has on other people, too."

As an aspiring attorney, Michelle has been studying this stuff in university for the past few years. She's destined to graduate soon, and aside from this sort of talk, it's the only other thing she speaks about. Still, I can't believe she's refusing to help.

"As an attorney, aren't you legally supposed to do the right thing in a case like this?" I ask her. She's studying this stuff. It should be at the top of her brain. If she wants to cheat the system already, then she won't be ethical in her career.

"I'm just looking at both angles, Chantel."

"Are you saying I'm just accusing J.R.?!" I ask, incredulous. "As in, you don't believe me? You know the same thing I do!"

"That's not what I'm saying, Chantel," she says. "Trust me, I am concerned, but Mom works with children. Imagine what would happen if something like that happened to her and she couldn't do that anymore. She'd be heartbroken, she may be already. She'd be out of work. She'd struggle to pay her bills and the most basic expenses. Without J.R. helping her with that, where would she be?" It's a rhetorical question, I know. She doesn't give me any time to answer it. "So please, just stay away from this, Chantel. Okay?"

I laugh into the phone. A disbelieving chuckle. There's no doubt in my mind that Michelle can hear. She just doesn't say anything. I shake my head.

"Stay away?" I question, as if it's crazy that she would even suggest that.

"Leave it be," she rephrases. "Let them be them. You don't have to visit them if you don't want to. You can stay behind if you want. Alexis can go see her cousins whenever. You don't need to be involved, Chantel." She pauses, then adds, "I'll look into putting Ashley and Ariel in therapy, and I'll pay for it myself, but I'm telling you, it's probably best if you let this go."

"You can't just fix these problems without getting to the root," I tell her, as if I'm giving her a lesson like we were kids. "I mean, put them in therapy all you want, I'm sure it would definitely help, but it doesn't guarantee any permanent solution. J.R. might molest other children if we don't do anything about *him*. For the record, I'm not worried about myself. I just—"

"I know," she interrupts. "You just want Roy and his kids and all the others that Mom's caring for to be safe. I just don't want you to make a stupid decision that I know you'll regret. So, just leave it, Chantel. Please. Let's not talk about this anymore."

The line goes silent. Dead. I bring the phone down from my ear, look at it. It is blank. Blank except for the apps on my home screen and the default background image that comes with all cell phones in the market.

I head back to my cubicle after getting a cup of steaming hot coffee and sit back behind the screen. Though I don't get back into my work like I want to, I just can't. I'm too busy thinking about the conversation I had with Michelle to dive back into the information from our clients, my analyses, and assigning the standard codes as per the classification system we use. Without her help, how can I possibly set things right in our family? How can I possibly show J.R. that there are consequences to his actions, to everything he has done? I don't know.

I am in the middle of thinking up other alternatives, other actions to take, when my phone pings. It has barely been ten minutes since Michelle hung up on me. I peek at the notification. It's a text message from Mom. I emit a silent groan at the thought, no matter how much I try to suppress it. I tap into it, put in my thumbprint to unlock the device. It reads:

> *Mom [8:14 p.m.]: What are you thinking Chantel?! Pressing charges against J.R.?! This is too far! I know you never really liked him, but I do, and I expect you to respect that.*

I don't even notice the way I grit my teeth at her words printed on the screen in the gray bubble until I see the bouncing ellipsis at the bottom of the screen on her side of the thread. She's still typing.

A minute later, another text comes through.

> *Mom [8:15 p.m.]: Michelle told you to leave it as it is. Roy told you to drop the matter a long time ago. I've told you the same! Every single one of us believes it's best to move forward from this, but you're the only one that wants to get stuck in the past. If that's the case, then I think it would be better if we don't speak.*

For a long time, the buzz of the office continues whirring past me, moving in a sort of blur, a fog. It isn't really that loud, distracting, or disorienting, but while staring at Mom's messages, it sure feels like it is.

I should've known Michelle told on me. Even to this day, she's still doing that. She just can't resist getting me into trouble. *What the hell,* I think, not at all for the first time. I click out of Mom's thread and select Michelle to type and text her about why she told Mom about our conversation. That's when I see it. At the bottom of the screen above the space where my message goes, it says three simple words that I never thought I would see. Perhaps I should've expected to see it, but I never did.

You've been blocked.

Chapter 11:
A Promise to Keep

If my family can't handle telling the open truth and standing up for injustices like the ones J.R. has presented, then I really couldn't care less. I'll act on my own accord. I'll talk to Dad, even though we don't have much of a relationship. I'll talk to the kids' parents about the dangers that their children are in. I'll talk to child services and try to get those kids in safer positions. I'll do whatever it takes to make this right. I've given this a lot of thought and I see no reason why I shouldn't do it.

So, that's exactly what I do.

Not just in the time I have today, or tomorrow, or the upcoming weekend, no. How I wish it would be as quick as that. How I wish this could all be solved with a snap. It's been a few weeks since I last spoke to Michelle. I haven't spoken to either of them, and at first, that bothered me. Now, I'm thinking that it isn't that bad. I have no one holding me back from doing what's right. There isn't anybody telling me to "let it be" or to "drop it" like I've been so frequently told. I have all the time in the world to set this right without anybody telling me otherwise, but still, I'd like this to be resolved as quickly as possible. The longer I wait, the higher the chance J.R. can screw up any other children's lives.

It takes a whole week for me to do it all, to put my plans into action.

The first thing I could think to do was call Dad and tell him everything about J.R., what he's done to us and to our family. He's always had the same number over the years, and when I turned 21, Mom gave it to me so that I could at least try to develop some form of relationship with him. It's been going okay I guess. I've been talking to him every week or so, I tell him about how Mom won't leave J.R. and do what's right. I tell him about how it's been affecting me. I tell him everything, and he gives me plenty of advice. Though when I get to the part where I want to go to the authorities about it, Dad seems hesitant.

"It might be trickier than it looks, Chantel," he said. He had thought J.R. was a pedophile, too, so many years ago, but unlike me, he never had the proof to confirm his suspicions. So, I almost wanted to agree with him until the confusion set in.

"Trickier?"

"What tangible evidence is there to show that J.R. is a bad man?" he asked. "Do you have anything to show them to prove he molested these people? Your brother? Your nephew? Nieces?"

Well, I didn't have anything to show him then. I still don't have any evidence to give, even after days of searching J.R.'s Facebook page and calling around to every victim of his I know.

I have nothing, nothing to prove that J.R. isn't what or who he says he is. I try not to get frustrated or upset, even though some days I want to just scream at the top of my lungs because of how difficult and how secretive he keeps his life. It doesn't make any of what I'm trying to do any easier to deal with.

It's not like I can really complain or spill all of this anger inside me to Alexis, I really don't want to have to do that, but sometimes I just don't know how else to handle all this. Lexie still doesn't know that I've decided to press on with my intentions even without the help of my family. She knows Michelle blocked me, literally all of them have but Mom, who I'm sure is considering doing so too. She might be still hesitating for all I know, but I haven't bothered to tell Alexis my plan of action. I know she'd probably side with her grandmother anyway, it's what everyone seems to be doing. I hate to hide it from her, but I just don't want this getting out until I have the evidence against J.R. *I'll tell her eventually,* I repeat to myself, *when it's right.*

Once, I did try to address the matter to the police, but they said exactly what Dad said. I need evidence. So, I left and tried elsewhere.

I tried contacting the FBI to see if they could do anything, investigate the matter or whatnot, see if there was anything they could uncover about J.R. that I can't. They told me the same, that they can't do it without probable cause. That was a real shame to hear a professional agency back down, and real discouraging, but I'm not giving up until I see J.R. face reasonable consequences. I promised myself that.

Now, I'm in the process of reaching out to the families of the kids that Mom and J.R. are watching. I've successfully spoken to four out of five parents of their children. Last is Charlotta, wife to Sebastian and mother of six-year-old Abigail.

I punch their number into the keypad of my phone and double check the post-it note to make sure I have it right. It is. So, I dial. My phone rings once, twice, three times, and just as I think it's going to send me to voicemail, the dial tone stops, and a lady's voice comes through, speaking gently, calmly, and politely. "Hello?"

"Hi, is this Charlotta?" I start.

"Yes, this is she," she answers. "Who is this?"

"It's Chantel, Victoria's eldest daughter," I say into the speaker. "I'm calling about your daughter. Abigail, is it?"

"What about Abby?"

"Well, I just wanted to let you know that my mom, your daycare sitter for her, is involved with a child molester. His name's J.R.—"

"Oh, J.R.!" she jumps in. "I met him when I went to pick up Abby a few times. He's very nice. I don't think there's anything to worry about with him, darling."

"Yeah, that's where I think you might be wrong," I counter, my teeth gritted and mind repulsed at the thought that she called him *nice*. "See, he's already groped my brother and my brother's kids, and last week, I got a face book call from another parent of a child my Mom's looking after that J.R. touched them too. I want to make sure Abby is safe and if so, I want to warn you."

She seems to chuckle at that, though brings the phone away from her ear because the sound is lessened. I wonder what is so funny, but in a matter of only five short seconds, I get my answer. "Oh, don't be crazy, dear," she says then. "Your mother told me it was nothing to worry about. I wouldn't be so dramatic."

I sigh, not bothering to dampen it or make it clear to her, just sigh. "I just wanted to let you know, that's all. Have a good rest of your day."

I end the call and place my phone face down on the granite kitchen counter at home. My heart seems to ache with a heavy loss just thinking again how hard Mom and everyone are trying to hide this, trying to keep J.R. safe and the victims unsafe. It's sick, and I'm embarrassed to even be related to them, to people that want to keep our family secrets as just that: secrets. Internally, I shake my head, though that motion transpires to the outside too.

Alexis is out with her friends, so I'm alone in the apartment. It is silent and getting dark. The time on the electric cooker reads 7:47 p.m. With the thought again roaming through my head of Alexis or the other kids being abused by that bastard, I pick up my phone once more and dial the only other number I have yet to call.

It rings.

When it stops, an automated voice comes through the receiver. It booms into my ear, robotic in its nature, "Welcome. Thank you for calling child services. Please, use the keypad to indicate what you need help with today." There is a short pause until the voice continues, "Press 1 if you have a child who is at risk of being abused or neglected. Press 2 if you wish to speak with one of our counsellors or support staff. Press 3 if you wish to report a case of domestic violence or sexual abuse. Press 4 if you would like access to some of our programs for—"

I hit three before the voice can go on, and when I do, it stops. Then says, "Please hold. We are transferring you to our customer report staff. This may take a minute."

So, I wait and sit at one of the stools behind the kitchen counter. A gentle soothing melody comes up while I rest the phone in front of me and put it on speakerphone. It sounds similar to the generic elevator music in our building, not playing any kind of song or lyrics, just playing a tune to pass the time.

A minute passes while I sip on my warm evening tea. It is enough to soothe me completely, almost seeming to stop my ruminating thoughts on the matter and take a deep, well-needed breath.

When the music stops and another voice comes on, this one is male, and I spark to attention. "Hi there, this is Patrick, crisis responder. How can I help you?"

"Hi there, my name's Chantel," I start simply, picking up the phone to my ear again and taking it off of the loudspeaker. "There's this man named J.R. in my family. He's living with my mom—I don't know who he is or if that's his real name—but he's a child molester. He touched my brother when he was eight and did the same with my nephew and nieces, and he tried to do the same to my daughter. Last week, I got a call from one of the parents of the kids that my Mom's babysitting, and she told me that J.R. might've done something to her son as well. I tried talking to the authorities about it, but they said they needed evidence to make a case for it. I don't have any evidence except that I know it's true. My mom even told me that she caught my nieces and nephew nude and one of my nieces was touching my nephew." I pause, wondering if I'm going too fast for him. "My mom runs a home daycare," I explain to him then, only now slowing down a little. "She's looking after around seven kids, pretty much all of them below five years old. I don't want them to be at risk like my brother and his kids.

The entire time I talk, I can hear the sound of keys on a keyboard clicking and clacking away on the other end. I assume Patrick is making notes of everything I've told him, and there's a part of me that smiles at that. That's more than anybody else has done, but I still worry he'll tell me the exact same thing: that he can't help without evidence.

"Is that all?" he asks genuinely. I can hear the friendliness in his tone. It's as evident as J.R.'s secrets are to me.

"Yes, that's everything," I answer. "I'm just worried for the rest of the kids my mom's taking care of. Please don't tell me you need evidence too."

The clanking of the keyboard seems to end when I tell him that, and he responds neutrally, professionally and neutrally, "I understand. Thank you for bringing this to our attention. What you told me near the end—that is a big red flag, about how your mother caught your nieces and nephew nude and touching one another. It's a sign that your nieces and nephew have been sexually abused. I'll bring this up with our staff and we'll let you know within the next week what our actions will be. Once again, I'm glad for the report. We take child safety very seriously over here."

"Thank you so much," I state. It sounds like they're taking this into consideration. That makes me happy for once. At least somebody is interested in protecting these children. All this time, I've been awaiting the moment when they'd tell me that they're unable to help for the exact same reasons, tell me that I need to provide evidence to make a case for it. I'd hate to hear of another organization ignoring them and sending the victims, possibly even future victims, to hell down the line.

"Though, I want to make it clear," Patrick begins again. "Our goal is to provide a safe and enriching environment to children of all ages. We work to protect the victims. If it's necessary to bring the police into the investigation, we will, but keeping children safe is our sole priority."

"Of course," I reply. "That's all I really need. Thank you."

"No problem," he says. "We'll be in touch shortly."

I pull the phone from my ear and hang up, and just a millisecond before my thumb hits the red end button, Patrick does it before me. I check the time. It reads 8:21 p.m.

The light from outside is nearly gone, only a dark blue in the sky's place. I leave the phone on the counter and head to the bathroom to shower. I'm supposed to pick up Alexis from her friend's place soon. So, I could use a quick rinse.

I turn the water up from lukewarm to steamy. Eventually the glass and the mirror fogs, and it feels good to let the warm water run over my skin and through my long dark hair. It's relaxing, somehow allowing me to forget everything going on and letting me accept the possibility of this shit being resolved soon.

Chapter 12:
Broken </3

> "It's easy to stand in the crowd, but it takes courage to stand alone."
>
> —Mahatma Gandhi

*** Ten Years Later; June 2021 ***

Most people think trauma can't be healed, as if it's just part of a victim's head. There are others who behave as though it doesn't exist at all. It's all just fake—fake experiences, fake memories, fake lies, fake everything. There's no such thing as PTSD, whether it's complex or acute. There's no such thing as abuse—verbal, physical, emotional, or sexual. There's no such thing as child molesters or pedophiles. As far as toxic elements of society are concerned, only soldiers in the military or Marines can ever have the excuse to claim they are traumatized or dysfunctional. Deep down, I know there are people that care about this issue, but apathy is what I see on a daily basis, everywhere, all the time.

Those that do understand how horrible trauma can be might allow sympathy and wish things were better for the victim of such a horrid event, but does anyone try to stop it from happening? Does anyone tend to care?

"Well, of course I care," says Sabrina, the therapist sitting in the gray armchair across from me, holding a yellow legal pad and silver pen in her hands. "My goal is to help people cope with difficult situations like you are, Chantel. Don't ever doubt that for a second. There's always somebody that cares, whether it seems like it or not."

Sabrina is a tall and older black woman with long straight black hair and dark brown eyes. She's dressed casually in blue jeans and a fancy blouse. I've been seeing her for the past few weeks because of everything going on since Michelle and I had that last phone call. Our relationship is fairly new. I may not have been touched or abused by J.R. like my brother has been, but that doesn't mean this shit is any easier to deal with.

I look around the small modern room. The walls are a plain and boring white and aside from the couch that I'm seated in and the matching armchair of hers across from me, there isn't much else. A tiny table for her notepad and pen to rest when her hands get tired of holding them, I suppose, along with a small glazed oak desk, in the corner. The entire place likely takes up a 12-foot width and 18-foot length, about the size of my apartment living room, any average living space. It's wide and open, and it probably would be comfortable too, if not for her watchful eyes.

Usually, I prefer not to seek professional help from others. I like doing things on my own, solving problems on my own, figuring out life on my own, being independent. Dad told me I should come here. He recommended this place specifically over others.

So, I did.

"She's a terrific therapist," he said over the phone yesterday. "I recommended her to your mother early after you were born. Give her a chance. She'll be able to help you through all this." So, I did. I guess Mom didn't, but I don't want to turn out like Mom. That's why I'm here now, and I'm not sure how glad I want to be.

"Sure," I say sarcastically, keeping my tone somewhat cold so that I don't scoff at her. "Because it's obvious that my whole family really cares. They all just want to protect that monster, and for what? Until when? Someone else gets hurt? I can't allow that."

"Love is a tricky thing, Chantel," Sabrina states. I can just tell she's checking me, observing me, as if my crossed arms will tell her something that I'm not. "Sometimes it feels great. Other times not so much. It can be blinding."

"You don't need to tell me..." I know how difficult love can be.

"Anyway, you want to run by me what's bothering you?" Sabrina asks, disrupting me from going down too far into the rabbit hole of my life. I'm glad for that. I don't want to think about my past again. "Is it about your Mom's boyfriend again? J.R. was his name?"

"Not exactly," I tell her immediately. "It's more than that now."

"What more is there?" Her tone is curious now, like she genuinely wants to know more and not just keep it for her records. I just don't know how much to tell her.

I wonder what Mom would say if she knew I was about to tell a therapist our secrets. Though it isn't long until I realize how much I don't care.

I haven't known Sabrina for very long. I've only been seeing her a few months. I'm nowhere close to telling her everything. I've been holding back from exposing my family's secrets until now, but today, I just don't know how to continue without telling her what's going on. I can't tell her what's going on or why if I don't tell her the source.

"Well," I start, biting my lip just wondering how she'll react. "The reason why I can't stand J.R. so much in the first place is because he's basically the one that ruined our whole family a long time ago. He abused my brother and then his kids, and he tried to touch my daughter too." I pause, watching her stare at me. "He's a pedophile, and I was too blind to see it, and because of that, everyone around me is suffering. The worst part is that no one cares. You can't tell anyone I told you."

"I won't, Chantel. It's against my agreement. As a therapist, I take confidentiality very seriously." So she's said, pretty much every week since we've met. "That sounds like it's been quite the issue for you."

"Oh, it has been," I continue, "and as if it couldn't get any worse, I'm the only one that wants to do anything about it. My entire family has blocked me because I kept pressing them to do the right thing, including my sister, Michelle; my nieces, Ashley and Ariel; my nephew, Chad; my aunties; and my Mom. I haven't spoken to any of them in years. Michelle told everyone in my family to stop talking to me and to stay away from me. Roy hates me. Ashley and Ariel are doing just fine without me. Chad probably wants nothing to do with me. Even Alexis has turned her back on me to side with my mom. They all think it's better to cover up the truth because if they don't, my mom will get into trouble, but that doesn't solve the victims' problems when it comes to being touched again. I've even tried to reach out to Ashley through her social media to tell her how sorry I am that J.R. did that to her, touched her so wrongly. I had to tell her how sorry I was for her grandmother not taking any interest in making things right. She saw my messages, but I never got a reply because Michelle told her to block me and not to talk to me again. My Mom told me that I wasn't allowed to come over to her place again for family dinners if J.R. would be there because she didn't want J.R. looking at me and not her. As if that even matters."

"That sounds like a lot to deal with," she says neutrally, and the lack of feeling in her voice almost makes me more upset. "I get that you must be feeling—"

"What?" I interrupt, arms crossed over my stomach. "Angry? Upset? Abandoned? No shit. My whole family would rather turn a blind eye than protect the actual victims of J.R.'s abusive behavior."

She writes a few things down on the notepad in her lap. I'm too far away to see for sure what she's writing down, though it looks to be only jot notes. I know I can ask her any time to see it. It's something else she constantly repeats at every one of our sessions.

"Don't be afraid to ask if you ever want to see my notes," she always says. "They are as much yours as they are mine." She does remind me of that again when she catches me looking from her to the paper.

I nod in acknowledgement like every other time but shake my head at the offer. I don't really care what she writes down. I know it's probably similar to what I'm saying aloud. It doesn't concern me.

What concerns me is the lives of every victim that J.R. has touched and how Michelle, Mom, and everybody I seem to know wants to do just the opposite of me. I'm concerned for the children in Mom's care and the possibilities of them going through the same.

"Yes, and it's completely normal to feel that way," she says. "It's expected. While it can be troubling, is there anything you are doing, or want to do, to make things better? If not with J.R. or your family, then within yourself?"

"Sure. I mean, I don't burn myself out about this. I relax when I can," I tell her, my muscles beginning to loosen and tension starting to dissipate. "I journal like you told me to do every night and talk to friends about what's going on. They agree with me by the way, but sometimes I feel like no matter how hard I try, things will never get resolved. As far as I know, nothing has been done. Mom is probably still living with that monster, and child services probably never interviewed them and the kids in their care. It's been ten years, and I still feel like nothing's changed. All I can do is hope the victims are somewhere safer than they were when in my mom's care, but the fact that Alexis left me too, probably living with my Mom and J.R. still, I don't know… It still hurts."

"I understand," Sabrina notes with a touch of remorse for me. "I'm so sorry you feel this way. Do you ever regret doing what you did?"

"That's the thing," I say. "I don't regret anything I've done to protect those kids. I would've done it anyway even if I knew everyone in my life would leave me for it. I just don't understand why they're so keen on hiding it."

A moment of silence passes, a silence awkward enough that I can practically feel the time ticking by. Like a bomb threatening to go off inside me, pressuring me until explosion. Sabrina watches me. I lean back against the couch and stretch my legs over the white fluffy rug, trying not to give a care because I know it's easier that way.

"Trauma can be difficult to process at times, Chantel," she says then at last. "I'm sure you know what I mean." Of course I do. I nod along with her. "There will be times where it can be a lot to deal with, which is why some people resort to or disassociating and avoiding certain situations. It may remind them of the trauma they've experienced. Have you been avoiding anything like that?"

It was early into our first few sessions that she explained to me what trauma is. She says that according to the Diagnostic and Statistical Manual of Mental Disorders (DSM for short), there is such a thing as acute stress disorder (ASD) and post-traumatic stress disorder (PTSD). Though, when I think of PTSD, I can't help but think of soldiers coming back from war and disregard it completely. She says that acute trauma is usually the cause of having lived through a traumatic event where your life was in danger or in threat of danger but only occurring within the first month. PTSD, on the other hand, lasts for much longer; as in six months or more. As far as I understand, they are pretty much the same except for the time period they last. They both result from a major stress-inducing event, give feelings of intense anxiety, disconnection from the world and yourself, repeating nightmares, trouble concentrating, and the symptom I'm least surprised about: flashbacks. Although I have never experienced anything of that sort, I do remember Roy telling me about some of those, particularly nightmares and flashbacks. He's also distant a lot of the time and doesn't want to interact with anybody, which I guess has to do with a disconnection or dissociative episode. With trauma due to sexual abuse and assault, Sabrina also told me that anger issues, withdrawal from once-enjoyed activities, loss of appetite, and difficulty sleeping or focusing are all classified under symptoms of trauma, all of which Roy has experienced, and probably still is.

Me though? This shit with J.R. in my family may be a lot to deal with at times, but I don't think I've ever avoided anything as a means to escape. There were times where I've most definitely hesitated to speak out about it, especially after what Mom and Michelle told me throughout my life, but it's nothing worth noting. I don't have flashbacks like Roy did. I don't get nightmares at night about J.R. I hardly ever get bad dreams at all or frequent anxiety attacks or anything.

I guess I have been slightly avoidant about that, even with Alexis. Most of the time, I do call and message her, even though she never responds. However, I haven't pressed her about moving in with me again. She was supposed to move in with me months ago, in March, but hasn't. I haven't even asked her why. I just assumed it was Mom's doing. Mom and Michelle's only way of getting back at me is to turn my own daughter against me, and sometimes that's what hurts me the most— more than all the hidden truths. But with regards to finding someone else...

"I don't know," I answer. "I guess I have been a tad avoidant when it comes to Alexis. I don't even intend to be. It's just that—I think my Mom probably got inside her head. Alexis doesn't usually think for herself. She's a bit dumb in that regard. She's easily swayed, especially by my mom. She practically idolizes her Aunt Michelle. Part of me just doesn't want to deal with that."

"That's understandable," Sabrina says. "But I hope you realize that the longer you put off speaking to her, or trying to, the worse your relationship can escalate with her."

"I know," I state. "I just don't know *how* to talk to her anymore."

"Have you tried messaging her? Or calling—"

"It's not that," I interrupt. "It's just—she thinks like my sister now. Whatever Michelle says, she agrees with, even if it doesn't make much sense. So, trying to convince Alexis otherwise is like trying to convince my sister first, and I don't know how possible that is. It just seems like my mom and Michelle are slowly turning everybody to their side. I'm the only one that sees the truth anymore, and I feel like that's why any of this is happening because I keep making it a bigger deal than it is and getting our family into more and more drama."

"You feel guilty for what happened to your brother?" she asks.

"How could I not?" I say immediately. "I was supposed to protect him all those years ago, and I didn't. J.R. hurt him, and I wasn't there to defend my little brother. He shut me out of his life because of that and I don't think I'll ever be able to live with myself."

Sabrina nods like she understands, but she doesn't. How can she? She watches me like a hawk, and usually that would bother me, but for some reason it doesn't.

"It's okay to feel guilty," she says then. "It doesn't always mean you're doing something wrong. In fact, I believe you're doing everything right."

"I keep trying to tell myself that," I say. "But I don't know. It still hurts. To think that everyone in my family is doing the opposite of me, the very opposite—and that's hiding it—and they're trying so hard. I just don't see the use in it all. I don't think they should, and I'm tired of remembering how related to them I am. I just want to get away from them all, get away from all of this. I don't even want to live in the same state as them anymore. I don't want to be anywhere near them, but it feels like I don't have a choice."

"We all have choices, Chantel," Sabrina tells me. "All of us. We're all capable of making decisions, whether they are good or bad, and we all think they are good unless someone tells us otherwise. So, why don't you?"

Why don't I? That's a good question. "I don't know," I reply. "I have enough money. I'm fully capable of relocating elsewhere far away from all this shit. Far away from *him*. I could probably use a fresh start, more or less."

"Right. So, why not?" Sabrina responds after making a few more notes down on her lap. "You never know what the future holds. It can change in a moment's notice."

"Nothing seemed to change within the last ten years." For all I know, everything is still the same. My mom is still probably sleeping with that monster, my nieces and nephew are still being touched, child services probably doesn't care, Roy and Michelle and my aunties still hate me—they're all pathetic. I know that for a fact. I don't talk to any of my family like I used to anymore, and for once, I'm glad about that. I don't even bother trying to reach Alexis anymore. So, nothing has really changed." I pause, think, then decide on sharing. "And—I don't know which is worse: knowing the truth about my family's lies or knowing that my own daughter won't talk to me either because of this. I'm not the monster. It's J.R."

"Who knows?" she says casually with a light shrug, finally dropping her pad and pen to the table. "Maybe one day, your mother will change. Maybe one day, J.R. will change—"

"Ha—" I interject. "I doubt it."

"Why's that?"

"Abusers abuse," I answer. "That's just what they do. I don't know why they do it, they just do. It's like an addiction in my eyes. They can't freaking stop." I pause. "My mom will always be a pathological liar that doesn't care about her kids or grandkids. Michelle too. She's in the perfect career for it, at least. I mean, an attorney? I bet she lies all the time to protect the accused. I don't see any of my family changing or accepting the truth any time soon. I don't count on it, and that's what upsets me more."

"I suggest you have a little faith, Chantel," she says. "The future remains unpredictable, and that's a good thing. It could change tomorrow or next week or maybe a month. Nothing ever lasts forever. You just need to stick with it. Are you writing in your journal? I think it will help release all these suppressed emotions."

"Not as often as I planned to," I admit. "I don't know, time just gets away from me sometimes, thinking about…all of this."

"Alright, here's your homework to complete before we meet next week," Sabrina states. "Keep writing in your journal, whatever comes up, and maybe let's reach out to a friend to get their opinion on moving out. Better yet, why not try to connect with your brother? It seems he is the root of some of what's stirring inside you. Maybe a heart-to-heart with him will help both of you feel better. Is that possible at all?"

"I guess I can try," I reply nonchalantly. "Thanks."

"No problem," Sabrina says and smiles. I stand, head out to where the front desk is, and pay my fee. The lady receptionist says it's a total of $180. She's an older woman, most likely middle-aged, and white skinned like many others in this part of Missouri.

So, I pull out my wallet from my blush pink handbag and pay the amount before waving her a genuine goodbye. Then leave to go home.

It's nearly dinner. The time reads 6:37 p.m. It takes until 7:15 to get back to the apartment, and just as I pull into the lot, I get a text message. My phone pings next to me in the empty passenger seat of the white four-seater vehicle. It's nothing but the default tone. The name displays Roy, which I find surprising. I haven't been close with him for years, at least since we were kids. I haven't even seen him since he moved out of Mom's place to live with his dad. We talk occasionally on the phone, but it isn't fun and happy talk like before. I think it's because part of him is still mad at me.

I find it odd that just as Sabrina suggested we see each other is the time he decides to reach out. Maybe he's not mad enough to block me like everyone else. His text message simply says:

Roy [7:48 p.m.]: Hey, want to come over this weekend?

I put the car in park in my usual designated parking spot and reach for the phone beside me, pull open the chat thread and type out my reply:

Me [7:48 p.m.]: Hey, sure. Ur not still mad at me?

Roy [7:48 p.m.]: No. I get it. I'm actually glad that you never shut up about all this.

Then another message comes through immediately after, reading:

Roy [7:48 p.m.]: I thought we could get together soon and talk. Catch up or whatever. It's been a while since I saw you, and I'd like to, I guess. Is that OK?

Roy and I have been on the greatest terms lately. We talk occasionally over the phone, but I've never been to his house, and he's never been to mine. I think he preferred it that way. I've just been waiting for him to say otherwise. Overall, he seems better than he was when we were kids. He's 33 now and has his own place. The last time we talked was a few weeks ago after a usual argument broke out between us about me spreading truths. He's never been really happy about that and what I do. I feel bad for not texting him sooner other than apologies, but I was worried he was still mad at me and would cut me out again like everyone else. Roy is the only person left who hasn't. So I wonder, why now? Why does he want to meet up this weekend? What's changed? I reply:

Me [7:52 p.m.]: Sure. Why?

Roy [7:52 p.m.]: No reason. I just think it'd be great to see you.

So, with a minute of thought, I type back a reply, reading a very simple *OK*.

Roy sends me a simple ordinary smiley face, the colon and closed bracket in text, and at 7:54 p.m. he sends another with his address and a time: 8410 Caroline Street at 5 p.m.

Then, I leave the phone on the kitchen counter and pull out the leftover food from the old white fridge. The magnetic door is littered with papers and magnets holding them up. Calendars, post-it notes of important dates, events set in the future and even from the past that I haven't removed. I tear off the old date of a gathering with one of my old high school friends. With a pan, I pour out the excess rice from the container and turn on the stove. While letting that heat up, I pull out some assorted vegetables to mix in with it too.

A couple of minutes pass in silence, nothing but the stovetop heating the pan of cold vegetables and bringing it to a satisfying sizzle when it comes to the right temperature.

When it's ready, I take the plate of food, pour myself a glass of red wine, and sit down on the sofa to watch one of my favorite movies packed full of suspense and late night thrills. The food doesn't taste bad or old. It tastes like it did yesterday. Rice, baked chicken, and the new soft veggies. With it, I enjoy the quiet of my phone and the sound of the movie while a yawn escapes my lips midway through the meal.

After the credits, I fall asleep with my head on the pillow to the right of the couch. The bare plate rests peacefully on the glass coffee table in front of me. I dream about Dad, Mom, Michelle, and Roy. I don't dream about J.R. I dream of a happy family like it never existed before. The first paradise, and inside, the entire time I walk through it like a spectator at a football game. I can feel myself tear-up deep under my bones. They are happy tears, but still tears.

Who Are We

We're no longer on the yellow brick road.
Where we're headed, only the devil knows.
For all the heartless and brainless in our group,
We'll never know how low they'll swoop.

To our mother, like the tin man looking for a heart,
Oh, how she's failed to protect us from the start.
And as her awareness slowly slips away,
There is no right or wrong in what she says.

Alexis is the scarecrow.
For selfishness is all she knows.
She searches for a brain,
Only thinking of herself, everything in vain.

As the cowardly lion, Michelle roars.
Except she doesn't walk on all fours.

TURNING A BLIND EYE

She lacks the courage to do the good thing,
To our mother's words, she protects and clings.

They all sing a liar's song,
For they are all wrong.
They fail to know what's true,
One day they'll learn…they always do.

Chapter 13:
Advice for Parents

There are rules for bringing up children in a healthy living environment. Not all of them are stated in any book, magazine, or newspaper, but they exist. They must be followed, or else it can lead children into unhealthy lifestyles and set them off on a detrimental path. Parents need to understand this, myself included.

I've learned a lot over the years about parenting and bringing up children, mostly from my own experiences and the mistakes that Mom has made and crimes J.R. has committed. I had to learn it all on the fly. I never read any parenting books or talked to life coaches. I had to figure it out on my own and at a young age. In the beginning, I didn't think it was fair. I had to learn those rules, the easiest way or hardest way, as quickly as I could for the sake of Alexis.

While everything might seem fine for Ashley, Ariel, and Chad, it isn't. They are moving through life completely blinded to how they feel and what J.R. did. They don't think of it as bad or good, just know that it happened. J.R. violated them in a way he shouldn't have, and I don't really care whether Chad and the girls adapt to it or not. The point is it happened, and they're forced to just move on from it because they don't see much other choice. It's important to see how messed up this is.

Kids need to learn the difference between good and bad touch. They need to know that having anybody touch them inappropriately is a form of abuse. Mom might not understand that, but I do. She's irresponsible and uncaring and blinded by her love for a pedophile, but I'm not. So it's up to me to make the better of all this. This doesn't have to happen again to anyone.

So, that's why I'm telling this story now. My story is more than just a story. It's reality. No matter how tough or vulgar or demeaning it may seem, this shit happens. It happens to families all around the world. Molesters like J.R. are just waiting to exploit people, even children, for their own twisted pleasure, but it doesn't need to happen.

This bit is here to give parents of any age, and victims all the same, rules to follow to avoid what happened to me.

Rule #1: Keep an eye on your kids.

Pay attention to the red flags your children give out. They'll do it unintentionally, so they'll need you to decipher them on your own. Red flags are very clear warning signs and symptoms to show that a child has been sexually abused, or perhaps even abused in other ways—verbally or physically. We need to keep an eye out for them.

When I called child services all those months ago, Patrick told me that catching a child nude and touching themselves or touching their siblings was a big red flag. It indicates sexual behavior because most likely they have been sexually attacked by someone else, which was the case for Ashley and Chad. It makes sense that they'd replicate what happened to them with each other.

Even if there aren't any warning signs, my point still stands. We, as parents, need to watch out for these red flags since they can greatly impact a child's life and future. It can show us whether or not a child is struggling like Roy has been all this time. Red flags are called red flags because they are dangerous. Most parents don't think so. They may think nothing of it. However, over time, it affects the child's behavior dramatically. Roy used to be a friendly, happy kid. After J.R. happened, he turned out to be the complete opposite in a way. Imagine that. How do you go from being happy, nice, and friendly all the time, always wanting to have fun, to reserved, quiet and shy, and lashing out at pretty much everyone you love? I don't know. If that's not proof that inattentiveness can lead down a dark path, I don't know what is.

In addition to initiating sexual behaviors on their own or with others' persistence, there are other flags to look out for. If a child shows changes in mood, for instance, or are irritable or angry all the time, that is something parents need to be made aware of. Loss of appetite, trouble sleeping, lack of interest in activities they used to enjoy. While these can be signs of other mental health related issues at the same time, such as depression, all of these signs will show that a child is experiencing something painful. Harming or cutting themselves especially is something that's also clearly identifiable. If they have cuts or scars on their arms, calves, or stomach, or if they refuse to unclothe to jump into a pool on a hot summer's day because they're at risk of revealing those scars. If they refuse to be alone with a certain person, whether they tell you so or not, as Roy was with J.R. and still is. These are signs. Aggressive actions count too.

I remember telling Sabrina one day that Roy once pulled a loaded gun on Mom and J.R. It was a while ago, when Roy was in high school, I believe. Alexis was in grade school and living with Mom while I was out trying to find us a decent living. I wasn't in the house then, but when Mom told me about what happened, I was furious. Upset and scared and confused, but mostly terrified. To think that Roy had a weapon from God-knows-where, though I always assumed he got it from—or *because of*—the older boys at school, it was scary to think that he would do such a thing. I didn't care what made him do it or who was behind it, whether it was the drugs he shared with his older friends or not, but the point is, it happened. It happened and Alexis was at risk all because Mom couldn't stand to step up or speak out for Roy and instead chose to hide J.R.'s actions to keep her *lover* safe, not our family.

This also includes other mental health related conditions and symptoms. If a child experiences anxiety (sometimes to the extreme) or depression after a run-in with a sexual predator, there are similar signs to be aware of. They might not want to be around a person or multiple people. Anxiety is a survival instinct in that regard. It protects them from being abused again, whether they know it or not. The shaky hands, tapping feet, difficulty breathing, eating, sleeping, or focusing. These are signs that a child does not want to be around a particular person or doesn't want to be touched a certain way or talked to in a certain tone, and that they may prefer to be left alone. When I talked to Roy a few days after he came home that day the first few days that he started to change, I tried to hold his shoulder to get his attention. He seemed distant, and I wanted him to know that I was always going to be there for him, that I wanted him to tell me what was going on, even though I could see how hesitant he was. As soon as I reached out to him, he flinched on my contact. It was like he was scared all of a sudden—scared of *me*, which at the time, I didn't understand. Now, I realize he really was afraid because it must've reminded him of J.R. So, especially if a child suddenly shows symptoms of restlessness and fear, or feelings of intense sadness and hopelessness when they wouldn't normally struggle with these things, it can clue us in. It's best not to ignore it, I found. I should've questioned Roy's actions back then and been more serious and concerned about it. Maybe then, things could've been different.

Rule #2: If a child is acting out, there is a reason.

Everything happens for a reason. It's a famous saying. I believe this to be true. I believe that every cruel, twisted, or good event comes to us on purpose. It might be to test us, teach us a lesson, or simply experience something new. Whatever it may be, we might not know what that purpose is, but God does, and He watches us react to it. So, in the end, we need to learn to accept this and identify what that reason is.

Now, that isn't to say that J.R.'s actions happened because they needed to. That's fucked up and he needs to pay the consequences. Mom and him both do. I've learned that with Alexis over the years. Over time, I've seen consequences with Roy, and later Chad, Ashley, and Ariel all thanks to inaction and the dismissal of the wrongs done to them. We need to be curious about their behavior, no matter if it's good or bad. Even if it might be hard, we can't afford to hold judgment based on what we see. Simply observe, process, and act.

Whenever Roy lashed out or screamed, when Ashley touched Chad, or whenever Ariel wanted to be alone with J.R., question it. *Why would they want those things? Why would they behave like that?* I used to think that all the time, and sometimes still do. It's strange. It's abnormal. It means something, it has to. These are nothing but simple, honest, and genuine questions that allow us parents to dig deeper, maybe even confront our children directly or reach out to a loved one and ask them for an explanation. There might be something physically going on in the child, or emotionally, or psychologically. Though sometimes it isn't easy to find an answer, and that has to be okay. Whether we get a reason or not, we can't do what Mom has always done, which is ignore it and sweep it under the rug. That leads us to the next rule.

Rule #3: Accept your children for who they are; don't ignore them.

Mom's biggest mistake was choosing to ignore her kids, maybe not so much her favorite child, Michelle, but Roy and I. Especially Roy and his kids soon after. She decided that it was best to pretend as if none of it ever happened to her youngest child and grandchildren. Even when Mom told me that she caught Ashley touching her brother, she seemed somehow fine with it. She wasn't interested in bringing a light to the matter. She just let it slide. Whenever I tried to speak up about it, she acted as though nothing was wrong. "Let it be," she kept telling me. I don't know what led her to do it or what made her not care, but I won't make her same mistakes. I don't want other parents to either.

Ignoring your child is never okay, in any sense or form. I was lucky to be able to build a relationship with Dad again when I was 21, but at that point, it was awkward. Now, it may be all good, but I have no memories of the "father-daughter" relationship other people have when they're growing up. There was a time where I thought that was my fault. I thought I was the reason that Dad left, that he just didn't want to take care of me or didn't want me in his life even though Mom made clear to me that it was Dad who didn't want to support us. Obviously, now I see that's not true, but in the past, it wasn't healthy for me.

Neglect brings on a lot of shame and guilt for no reason. It doesn't matter if parents are physically absent or emotionally absent or just aren't there, period. Any form of neglect is harmful to a child. I grew up thinking that without Dad, I'd never know what to look for in men, and that might be the reason why I still don't have a strong relationship with one to this day, even with Austin and Chase, two men I've met recently and started dating. Roy grew up thinking that Mom didn't love him because she never did anything to soothe his hurt feelings. He used to tell me that all the time. "Mom doesn't love me," were his exact words. I remember them like they haven't left my mind. Chad probably thinks the same, which is why he's a quiet kid. Ashley and Ariel, I honestly don't know what to think of them. They make it seem like what happened was no big deal. Like they're adjusting—a gentle breeze blowing through the wind, not worrying about where it's going or why. Forcing the child to ignore the event of their lost innocence isn't right either. They are just becoming less of who they are, less of the person we made and want them to be.

So, we need to bring these sorts of difficult topics to light and address the changes in our children's behavior as we see them. Remember, if something is difficult for you to speak about, chances are good it's difficult for your child to speak about it, too. Chances are, they don't want to talk about it either. Trauma, specifically abuse, isn't something that we're able to easily shine a light on, but we need to try. When I was asking Alexis if J.R. touched her like he did her cousins and uncle, it was awkward, but I had to do it. I had to know if that monster was involved with my daughter. It was about safety, assurance, and it would let me assess how good or bad of a parent I was.

So, we need to try if we want to spark change.

Rule #4: Talk to your children about their red flags if you find any.

If you see that your child does have changes in their academic performance or is wetting the bed when they have never done so before, ask them about it in a calm and cool way. Don't let it slide because "they're only seven, six, or five." Ask because it doesn't hurt to ask. If you're gentle about it, they won't mind. They'll probably think of it as a regular conversation, an awkward conversation, but a conversation, nonetheless. I just wish I was able to do so with Roy or Chad when I had the chance. They have both been bed-wetters after the incidents with J.R., and I thought nothing of it. I hate that I never looked deeper and just tried to shrug it off. Ignoring something is turning a blind eye. It is not eliminating the problem. It's sweeping the problem under the rug and letting it intensify. This is unhealthy for the child, and even to parents down the road.

Since Mom started keeping a lid on J.R.'s behavior with Roy, Roy hasn't spoken to her as much as he did. He'd always been a happy, friendly, giddy kid, and it pains me to see that side of him die because of Mom dismissing his trauma. It isn't fair. I have to deal with the fact that every one of the victims that has been affected by my twisted family doesn't want me around, doesn't want to talk to me, doesn't want me to even get involved because they were taught to hide their problems, not solve them.

That is not the way. It sucks for everybody involved, as it should be, and if we're going to stop it from happening, we can't just let it go unspoken. As horrible as it can be that it occurred, it needs to be talked about. At the same time, it's important to make sure we don't normalize it because sexual abuse and assault should not be normalized.

Rule #5: If a child has been sexually abused, put them in therapy.

It's as simple as that. If we don't, it can possibly lead those abused children to later become pedophiles in the future, and the cycle will just continue. Going to therapy every week or month can help the child cope with what has happened to them. It can help them understand the difference between right and wrong touch, and that their experience was *wrong.* Therapy gives us a chance to work through the trauma instead of ruminating in it and holding onto it—holding onto the grudge.

Since Chad is going to therapy, he should be much better off after the situation that happened to him with J.R. He'll grow to understand triumphs and aches and hopefully, because of that, he won't put the same aches and pains onto others because he'll have healed through them. I have to hope that the girls realize the same, whether on their own or with a therapist in the future.

Even myself. I might not have had J.R. touch or abuse me directly, but seeing all this occur around me, it does more than simply open my eyes. It makes my own heart ache for the people, children, and the lives that J.R. had to ruin. I couldn't live with the fact that if I had noticed how crude and disgusting J.R. was earlier and done something then, maybe I could've prevented him getting to my nephew, nieces, or Mom's daycare kids. I thought it was no big deal, so I kept thinking life was normal. Because of that, Roy's children are suffering the same consequences that he had undergone a long time ago, and this time, they don't have a dad to turn to for support nor a mom. All Ash, Ariel, and Chad have is a faulty grandmother who likes to keep problems invisible and discouraging them from coming to me for help.

Sabrina has tried to tell me that it's not my fault our family trauma keeps repeating. She tells me to journal and meditate about it, to take deep breaths when my mind starts to go down that rabbit hole. Sometimes it works, and it seems to calm me. Sometimes, it doesn't at all. Sometimes the guilt and shame is all I feel, and the fact that I am the cause of my nephew's and nieces' trauma is as clear as a cloudless day. Deep down, I know all of this is J.R.'s fault, not mine, but there are days where I am really not sure. It's still something I'm trying to work on to this day.

Rule #6: Be consistent in how you parent. (Stoppler, n.d., para. 15)

Whatever you decide to do, however you treat your kids because of this book, be sure that your behavior is as consistent as theirs. Children learn from behaviors, from things we practice day in and day out, our daily routines and the things we do, how we handle decisions and ourselves in given situations. Adults are their role models, and they tend to copy what we do, whether they know it or not. That saying, "Do as I say, not as I do," doesn't help either of us out very much because it is only one way. You are not setting an example for your kids; you are telling them to behave better than you do without showing them what better means. Children mirror what they see. It's how they learn right from wrong because ideally children get to know what is right for them and others purely based on what they see around them.

With regards to Ashley and Ariel, they see behavior like J.R.'s actions toward them, and they think it's okay to be treated like that. They think that kind of touch is okay. That's likely one of the reasons why Mom caught two of them nude together, touching each other. It was learned and practiced before. They don't understand how wrong it is because someone older did it to them. It might not come from their parents, but they've seen it performed.

It doesn't matter if it's practicing consistency through physical habits like showering and getting ready for school, or emotional habits like letting your kid cry and comforting them when needed, or mental habits like doing your best to understand your child, what they're thinking and feeling inside. A child will pick up on anything that you do and attempt to mimic the way you do things for the same reasons as long as they're young enough to do so. Stick to your good nature, and your kids will stick to it too.

Rule #7: Avoid severe punishments. (Stoppler, n.d., para. 16)

Laurence Steinberg, an American professor of psychology specialized in child and adolescent development, once said, "Children who are spanked, hit, or slapped are more prone to fighting with other children. They are more likely to be bullies and more likely to use aggression to solve disputes with others."

Beating a child is never okay, I don't care what anybody else says. Mom has always been physically and verbally abusive. It's the entire reason why I don't hit Alexis. I know what it's like. I just don't believe hitting a child will make them behave any better. Nobody should ever be getting away with spanking a child. There are other ways to deal with misbehavior. You may be mad, and that's normal, there are healthier ways to discipline children, like talking with them, giving them a time-out, or taking away privileges like screen time or sweets. Kids care about those things, and they'll do anything to make sure they aren't taken away. While it's true that every child is different and some of them react heavily to these consequences while some don't react much at all, the latter is no excuse to resort to any kind of physical violence on the kid. There is always another, safer resolution.

Rule #8: Communicate with your child.

In my opinion, there can never be enough communication between a child and parent. Talk to them as much as you want, and it will be good for them. Explain yourself whenever you make a decision, however briefly or in depth you want to go. If a child asks why you are doing something one way and not another, answer them honestly and genuinely. Don't ignore them or tell them you're busy. Don't compromise and say you'll explain later and then forget about the matter entirely. While it may be hard to explain yourself in a way for your little one to understand, it is worth a try.

Without communication, parents and kids may as well be living two separate lives. I don't think any parent plans that originally when they have kids. We want to feel connected to them even when they leave us to live their own lives. We'll call and message them to see how they're doing because we want that motherly or fatherly connection with our loved one. It's the same with any family member or friend.

Rule #9: Don't bribe your kids!

Bribing your kids to get them to do something or hide something is similar to ignoring them. Mom should never have bribed Roy and given him hush money to keep silent about what J.R. did to him. Michelle shouldn't have either, but they did it to protect the man responsible, and that's disgusting. I hope no one ever does the same.

It doesn't even have to be with money. I know some parents like to use other things—phones, toys, TV—to get their children to do things that they've been avoiding, but I don't believe it's the best way. It's pretty close to being the exact same thing. You are just using something else instead of money. While it is better than hitting the child if the task doesn't get done, I believe there are healthier ways to handle that. Talking to them and explaining why they need to behave a certain way or do a certain job can work better than expected. Not shouting or yelling in anger, but a firm tone. I've done so with Alexis while she was growing up because I had to, and perhaps I got lucky because she's never really been the rebellious type, but it did work.

Though I'm sure there'll be more rules to parenting to ensure that this doesn't happen again to anyone else, for now, this is what I've learned from watching it all spin around me for years on a repeating cycle. I hope to break that cycle. I plan on doing more than that.

I intend to break it, and these rules will help.

Chapter 14:

Fall Out

I head out of the apartment as soon as I'm done with my afternoon shower. I had to freshen up before going to see Roy. The time on my phone reads 3:46 p.m. I talked to Roy asking what time he wanted me to come and where to go, and he said 5 p.m. is fine and texted me the address. It's June 11th, and it'll take nearly a half hour to drive there. I'd like to get there early. So, by 4:15 p.m., I am out the door and in the car, driving down the freeway toward my little brother.

The road is busy at this time of day, which doesn't surprise me at all. Everybody is making their way home. There are trucks and motorcyclists and dozens upon dozens of cars. I drive at a steady 55 to 65 mph throughout the duration of the trip, slowing and stopping occasionally when the cars bunch up together. I'm at Roy's place in 45 minutes max, arriving at 5 p.m. sharp thanks to the evening traffic of everyone leaving work.

Roy has a nicer house in this area of Kansas City. It's suburban. The residential area is small, shops are close, everyone is out and about smiling, nodding, chatting with one another as if they were best friends. I marvel at it, and I can already tell it's a safe neighborhood at night. There probably aren't any drugs or gangs lurking about in between alleys or whatnot. Also, there are a lot more alleys compared to Mom's place. Most of the houses are unattached, not paired with another or a line. They are stand-alones. Roy's home has one car in front of it, a regular, black four-seater similar to mine sitting the single driveway, just a different make and model, and I can tell it's newer, very much so. I park beside it on the side of the road.

Then, I make my way up to the front porch—it's bigger than Mom's too—and I ring the bell. The doorbell at the very least sounds the same as any other I've rung. A default ding, high-pitched and demanding attention.

When Roy comes to answer the door, I don't even recognize him. I'm just—frozen and left staring at the man standing in front of me. He's way older and has changed so much compared to when I last saw him, which was about 20 years ago, and even though we've talked on the phone occasionally, and I've heard his grown up voice—a deeper and gruffer sounding voice with a tough demeanor—I haven't at all seen how his appearance has changed. His hair is grown out into low dreadlocks, but it still doesn't go past his shoulders, and I know if Mom were with him, she'd tell him to cut it. He's still thin but looks toned, like he's been working out. I look into his eyes, and they too look different. It's as if they're healed, if it weren't for the glimmer of nostalgia he gets under the evening light from seeing me.

"Hi, Chantel," he starts slowly, awkwardly. "Come on in."

"Hi," I reply just as simply, still a little too stunned to say much else. I step inside, remove my shoes at the door, and give him a look while he shuts it. "You look different—better, I mean, than the last time I saw you."

I smile, and he smiles small, one that I haven't seen in so long. I'll admit, the inside of his house looks pleasant, just as nice as Mom's place. "Thanks," Roy responds, and I can't help but wonder if that's all. I guess I never expected him to say much during my visit. I was prepared to do most of the talking. Roy leads me to the family room full of sofas and foldable chairs, the latter of which is leaning up against the back wall. The family room isn't far from the front door. It's just to the left. I sit on the largest sofa, and Roy sits in the single chair, then asks, "Can I get you anything to drink?"

"Just water would be nice," I manage to get out, speechless in his mannerisms. The last time I saw him, he was an angry hothead. Now he's calm and cool, maybe a little cold, but otherwise seemingly happy to see me in person after our brief calls.

Roy nods and retreats further into the house near the back, toward the kitchen I assume, and I wait patiently until he returns. It looks like he's doing well here for himself. I'm more glad than I thought I would be. I'm proud. In no time at all, Roy returns with a tall glass of water and sets it down on the glass table in front of us. I take my first sip and say thanks. Roy nods and starts us off, "What'd you want to talk about?"

I start us off slow and just ask him how he's been. Clearly better than the last time we've seen each other, but I want to know from him. He's polite about it, understanding. He answers honestly and gently without raising his voice and says he's been working as a mechanic in an auto repair shop for the past four years. I know he switched careers from technician to mechanic from our talks on the phone, and when I ask him if he enjoys it, he says he does. It shows. Roy looks happy here.

He asks me what I've been doing, and I tell him that too. I tell him how it's going at the Nivea Health Care and what it's like being an administrative manager: boring, but someone has to do it. I tell him about the last meeting with Sabrina the therapist, and he looks shocked to hear that I'm seeing a therapist.

"How come you're seeing a therapist?" he asks when I mention such a thing. "He—he's never done anything to you."

The entire time we talk, Roy won't say J.R.'s name out loud, which is about expected. I don't even want to think his name in my head. I don't even know if it's his real initials. The bastard has kept his life secret for so long.

"No, but it hurts to see everyone around me be victimized by him," I tell him. "I know, I was surprised too, but Sabrina said just because it didn't happen to me directly doesn't mean it can't still affect me. I guess it's been getting to me more than I like…"

Roy goes silent then, and the two of us sit in total stillness until, eventually, Roy apologizes. I tell him he doesn't need to, but he does anyway.

Then we move on to talking about our kids. Roy's kids and Alexis. I start with Alexis when Roy asks about her. I explain to him that she moved out of the apartment seven years ago to start a life of her own, just like I have on the phone—tell him that I think she's working her own job, but I don't know where or what exactly she's doing. Roy says that's good for her, but I don't know. "I'm pretty sure she's living with Mom and that freak," I tell Roy, twiddling my thumbs while holding on tight to the glass in my lap. "It's not that I'm worried about her. I think Alexis is old enough to keep him away from her and all anyway, but still…"

"You never know what will go wrong…" Roy finishes for me. He knows exactly what I'm thinking and why it bothers me. Even after all this time we've been apart, he's still the little brother that gets me at his core, the little brother that used to team up with me whenever Michelle poked her head and made fun when we were kids before lying on us and getting us in trouble. The memory of who we were brings an inner smile to my lips. "Anyway, how have you been?" he asks. "Like, with personal connections? Did you end up finding another boyfriend?"

"Oh, I don't know yet," I answer, and at that, he looks confused. So I explain.

I tell him I've been dating. I met Austin and Chase at the local bar. I tell him Austin is a regional manager for a technology company and a few weeks after we started chatting and going out for coffee, I met Chase, who works for the FBI. Roy seems impressed at hearing about Chase's job title, and he even jokes, "Is he as good as in the movies?"

I chuckle at that and shrug. "Never seen him in action at his work. Maybe one day though." My relationship with Chase is newer than the one I have with Austin, and both are growing slowly and steadily. At this rate, I can't tell which one I'll end up with or if I'll end up dumping them both. Austin is slightly more handsome than Chase though, but Chase seems more intelligent and rational in the decisions he makes in his daily life. Austin feels like more of the outgoing charismatic type. So, I've made it a point to keep dating them both until one of them just clicks, hoping it will be that easy even though I know it won't be.

While I'm telling Roy about the two men that I recently met, I notice briefly that Roy is wearing a ring on his ring finger. It's a plain silver ring as far as I can see, and within seconds, Roy can see me eyeing it. When I smile and start to ask him about it, he just nods before I can finish and says, "Her name's Kisha, and we've known each other for five years. Been married for three."

"Wow!" I respond, completely impressed he was able to find love before me, as if it's one of our greatest childhood competitions. "That's great! I'm happy for you."

"Thanks," he replies. "We're not planning on having kids though. I don't want any more and neither does she."

"That's fine," I assure him because he sounds insecure about it. "Who said you need to have kids to be happy or find love? I think it's great that you were able to find someone anyway. Where is she now? I'd love to meet her."

Roy says she's at work, that she's a registered nurse and works a busy schedule today. It's Friday, so it's her busiest day, but he says that she'll be home by 9 p.m. tonight if I want to stay that late for when she arrives. So, I nod and stay. I have no problems with staying that late. "Does she know about Chad and the girls?"

"Of course," he says with a nod. "She says that one day, if I'm okay with seeing them again, she'll want to meet them. I don't plan on that happening any time soon though…"

I ask him why he thinks so, and he says he just isn't ready. I don't understand why. Why wouldn't he want to see his kids? I don't press him. I learned my lesson from the past. If Roy isn't ready to interact with Ashley, Ariel, or Chad, he isn't ready. I need to accept that.

So instead, I just fill him in on some updates about his kids that I think, maybe, he might be interested in at least. I let him know that Chad is seemingly gay, Ariel seemingly bisexual, and Ashley assumingly lesbian, but based on what she posts on social media, she appears to be confused. I tell him that I think their varied sexualities come from what J.R. did to them, though I don't know how true that is. Roy questions that, and I explain that Ariel apparently *likes* J.R., as in more than just her grandmother's boyfriend. I tell him what Mom told me, that Ariel tends to always be around him, following him, being right by his side, going out with him. It's like she's pretending to be his girlfriend, which I think is so messed up. Roy agrees with me. They are 50 years apart, more or less. It's weird and gross. I even tell him what Mom thinks about them all, that she doesn't like the fact that Ashley is a lesbian.

"Really?" Roy questions. He's just as surprised as I am.

"That's what she told me," I say. "But really, what can she possibly say?! It's her own damn negligence that made them that way. If J.R. just acted properly around those kids, or if Mom left him, then she'd have nothing to complain about."

"Isn't that also hypocritical?" Roy states. "I mean, *he's* bisexual too *and* a pedophile."

"Oh, 100%!" I reply. "She has no right to say that about either of your kids because she loves someone that's just the same!"

"That's fucked up," Roy says, and I nod along with him. "And you're sure child services didn't do anything about it?"

"Not that I know of," I confirm. "As far as I know, they interrogated them both, including the kids she's babysitting, but those two are still living together. I have no idea if she's still running a daycare. I even posted on Facebook warning parents not to send their kids to her because she's involved with an abuser, but no one seems to care."

"I know…" he says. "I saw the post and the responses. Some people are idiots."

"Only because they don't see the truth," I say. "Oh, and also because Mom's prices for babysitting are cheap, so it's easy for parents to compromise their child's safety when they're getting a cheap rate. I'm sure that doesn't help."

"True," Roy agrees, smiles, and we both laugh some more before Roy offers to order us some pizza for dinner. I nod and agree. Pizza would be great. So, he does.

He goes to grab his laptop and opens up the internet browser to our old favorite pizza restaurant. He orders an extra large beef pizza with extra cheese—he doesn't even need to ask. I offer to pay for him, but he refuses and pulls out his wallet anyway. So, I let him.

I've learned a lot about trauma over the years. One thing in particular is that survivors often want to feel in control. Roy is like that, has been and still is. I can tell. Whatever residue of trauma is still floating around in his head and heart, I'll give him as much control as he can possibly ask for, even if he doesn't ask for it directly.

Once the pizza is good and paid for and on its way into crafting and delivery, Roy offers to get me more water or another drink like soda. I shake my head and insist I refill my glass myself. He doesn't need to treat me while I'm here. We're brother and sister. Besides, I feel like I owe it to him for pushing his pain aside for so long instead of taking it more seriously like I am now. Roy allows me to, leads me into the kitchen, and I refill the glass from the tap.

We end up sitting down at the kitchen table and continuing our chat. It's a fancy kitchen and the table is spotless despite the pile of dirty dishes in the sink—they only take up about half the space. The table, dark brown, small, and round, is enough to seat up to four people, one on each side, while a gorgeous delicate chandelier dangles above us, sparkling little yellow lights. Roy sits across from me and I sit with my back to the black electric stove. During the wait, we talk about what's changed and what's old, what we miss the most from our childhood and don't. Even though we don't go into too much detail about the past, we both agree that we definitely don't miss getting in trouble because of Michelle, then being teased by her after. We mostly keep our eyes on the future. Roy tells me what he wants to do, settle down and enjoy life and try to be normal for once. I tell him what I want to do, maybe move away from it all and start fresh, find someone else like Roy did, and settle down somewhere away from the hustle and bustle of the city, or even a suburban place like here but farther away from J.R. and Mom.

Sooner or later, the doorbell rings, and Roy hurries to get it. I can hear the boy passing along the pizza on the porch even while I remain seated at the table, sipping my cool water with ease. I can smell the beef in the pizza as soon as Roy brings it in. It wafts throughout the entire house like perfume does when you apply the first puff. He sets it down and sits down again then opens it up. I ask him for plates, and he points to one of the top cupboards above the marble counter where a stack is practically waiting to be used. I pull out a couple of them and hand him one then reach for a slice for myself. He does the same and we eat.

It tastes as good as it smells. For our first slices or so, we don't say much, simply enjoying the food. By the time Roy reaches for another slice, we continue talking. We keep chatting in between bites and slices about various things that have happened to us during our time apart. Stupid things, silly things. We're halfway done in no time. The clock behind me on the oven display reads 8:06. I'm done with my third slice by the time my stomach tells me I'm full.

Only when I reach for my glass of water, almost empty again, does Roy start up in brand-new conversation. "So, I wanted to ask you," he says. "Why didn't you do anything about—uh—*him* when we were kids? Why'd you just continue like nothing happened?" That almost gets me to choke on my water.

I'm not sure what to say to that at first, but eventually the words come to me, one by one. "Roy, I didn't know what was going on. I was only 16. I tried to find out what happened that day you came back from John's house, believe me, I really tried. I asked Mom over and over, I asked Michelle, both of them, before and after I asked you the weekend we were by ourselves. Remember?"

"Yeah, but after that you didn't bother me anymore." He almost sounds like he's complaining. I don't understand why.

"You told me to drop it, so I did," I lie but instantly regret it. "I just—I don't know. I thought I was making too much of a big deal out of it."

Roy goes silent then, holding his pizza by the tip of the crust and picking at the tender dough while the rest sags on the messy plate.

"Still," he says. "You could've tried a little harder."

"Harder? How?"

"I don't know, but you could've done something else, anything to fix it," he says. "I know you saw Mom give me hush money every Wednesday after school. It was always the same amount. $100.00 dollars. You never bothered to ask what it was for or why she was doing it all of a sudden. Why didn't you?"

I'm not sure what to say to that. So I end up murmuring a weak, "I don't know…"

"Come on, Chantel!" he says then, louder now, that same old frustrated tone beginning to return. I thought he had lost it completely, but it sounds just as similar as the day I heard it last. "You can't expect me to believe that! That you honestly had no idea!"

"But I didn't," I say. I feel horrible all over again.

"Stop lying!" he shouts. "You knew! I know you knew! You just didn't want to do anything about it. Like Mom and Michelle. You wanted to hide what J.R. did, just like them!"

"Hide him?!" Now he has me yelling. "That's insane! I've been working my ass off to make sure that monster is put in his place!"

"Have you?" he counters. "Then why haven't you made any progress?"

"Because the damn police said I needed evidence to make a case against him. As in physical concrete evidence that they could use," I explain, trying to regain my calm composure by purposely lowering my voice. "I just didn't have any, and child services said they aim to protect the victims. I have no idea why he's still living with Mom or if they're still running the daycare. Really, I tried to do everything I can think of, Roy. That's the truth. Also, it doesn't help that you didn't come forward either. You could've chosen to speak out about it and take my side. I'm not blaming you. J.R. has silenced everybody. I'm just saying."

I can see the change on his face now. His features contort into an angry armadillo, hard and furious on the outside but easily hurt and broken on the inside. As much now as he use to be. I can see that through his eyes. They are like glass, brown and watery but crystal glass. All of a sudden it's like nothing has changed. Somehow my presence, my truth, made everything come back. The trauma—his trauma—worsened, and I just know he hates me just like he did 25 years ago. He thinks I did nothing, less than I should've done. He thinks I've always been working on Mom's side, not trying my hardest to bring that twisted man's acts to an end. He thinks I'm the cause of his pain, as much as Mom and Michelle are, as much as J.R. perhaps.

It's almost crystal clear to me now. He hates me. This rare nightly chat was going well, but it didn't take a whole lot to bring him back, make this new spin right back around and run again to the old one. The reality sets in.

Roy hates me. He hates me. Hates *me*. Is there anything I can say to change his mind? Anything I can think of to convince him otherwise? To show him that I really did do all that I can? I wrack my brain for anything I can use or tell him.

I come back empty and meet my brother's eyes, see the upset at his core, the clench of his jaw, the strength in his closed fist. Then he says something that I never expected him to say. Something that breaks me to a new level.

"Drink bleach, Chantel," he says, his tone cold, emotionless, but at the same time hurt and broken. I can tell he is just trying his hardest to hold himself together. "Just—leave. Get the fuck out of my house."

My heart, frozen as it may be, stares up at him. I want to say something, anything, but the words don't come. Roy's words are the only thing I hear, especially those first three. *Drink bleach, Chantel.* The way he even says my name makes it sound like I'm a curse. A curse for not trying harder, better, a curse for not doing something when I should've. His threat whispers in my mind on repeat. *Drink bleach, drink bleach, drink bleach.*

"Get out!" he yells, his voice now just a tad shaky.

Finally, I do. My body moves, drifts on its own. I grab my handbag and walk out.

Chapter 15:
After the Storm

I look through the contacts in my phone until I come across Christina's number. I tap her name, the phone takes me to her info, and I hit call. The phone rings. I can hear it in the receiver even while the thing remains down from my ear.

Once. Then twice. It is quiet in the apartment even though the TV. I have it turned to a low volume, just ten ticks on the remote. On the third ring, Christina picks up, and her voice comes through. I tap the button for the speakerphone, and she gets louder when I do.

"Hey, Chantel!" she starts. "Been a while. How're you doing?"

"Hey Christina," I reply. "Not too bad, not too bad. I thought I'd call to catch up. How's life in Texas? Is Christin adapting well?"

Christin was her 12-year-old son, named after his mother. It has been exactly ten years since they moved out of the state. I haven't spoken to either of them since then. Christin was just two years old at the time and Alexis was 16, hanging out with her friends. I still remember that day I saw her in person. She was young, cradling a baby and carrying him in a small stroller. Christin was wrapped in blankets and had a plushie bear lying next to him. It was a bright and sunny day. Summer weather. It's hard to believe it's been that long already.

"Oh, he's doing great. Gone into middle school and settled in well here," she says. "How are things back in Kansas City?"

Christina and her family decided to move to Texas for the sake of convenience for work with extended family there. As far as I know, the place that she's moved to in Houston is safer than the street that we grew up on.

"Essentially, could be doing better," I admit. "Remember J.R.?"

"That creepy man that kept sending you Valentine's Day gifts?"

"Yep," I confirm, a little embarrassed at the fact that he was creepy way back then, and I didn't think anything of it. "Well, turns out, he's creepy for a reason. He's an abuser, and not only that but a child molester too. He's been involved with my brother and all his kids and probably way more."

"Jeez, Chantel!" she exclaims. "Are you alright?"

"Fine," I lie nonchalantly. "At this point, I just want to get away from it all, you know? I was thinking about moving to a safer place, away from my family and away from *him*. I don't want to live anywhere near them. They're pathetic, and none of them have listened to me over the years whenever I told them to ditch that bastard."

"Oh! Come to Texas!" she says, suddenly overjoyed at the thought. "Houston, it's great here!"

"A whole different state?" I initially respond, only half aware of saying it out loud. "I've never been outside of Kansas City before, let alone the state altogether."

"Come on, it'll be fun, Chantel," she continues, trying to egg me on. "I'll be waiting for you at the airport. You can drive if you want! It's ten hours or so, without traffic of course, but you can stop by my place and stay with me until you find your own."

"That's a really generous offer, Christina," I tell her. "Thank you, but I don't know anything about Texas. I don't know how much safer it is over there or which place is better than others, what the economy is like or anything. I mean, you say all these great things about it, but I have to worry about so much if I move. I have to look into selling my apartment, finding a new place over there, plane tickets even, and probably way more that I'm forgetting. I guess I will get away from J.R. and my family, but there's so much else to consider. Like, what if I meet someone else just like *him*—"

"Hey slow down, Chantel," she interrupts me, and I realize how fast I was talking: very. "I'll help you! I'll even fly over there myself and help you out with selling that apartment of yours, or you know, we could just do it over the phone. I'll help you pack and everything. What do you say?"

"That's great and all, Christina," I start. I don't have to shut her down so soon. "Part of me really wants to look at my options first. I'll call you back in a few days or so, okay? We can talk all about Texas then. I just have a few things on my mind that I want to take care of first. Is that okay?"

"Sure, sure! No problem! I'll be here."

"Thank you."

TURNING A BLIND EYE

> ❝ *"The great thing in the world is not so much where we stand, as in what direction we are moving."*
>
> —OLIVER WENDALL HOLMES

So, a day passes by. Then another.

I talk to Dad about it, and he's just as enticed by the idea as I am. I tell him it's only to get away from J.R. because I don't want him anywhere near me, and he says it's a great idea. He says it multiple times during our call. He asks if I'll let him know where I settle in, the place, the neighborhood, and I tell him of course I'll give him the location. Dad is nothing like J.R. He's been the Dad that I always wanted growing up, and I'm glad I at least have him now to turn to for advice.

He tells me what I need to do, practically guides me through it. He gives me the addresses of the best real estate sites where I can buy the best affordable housing in Houston and tells me what to look out for and how to sell my own apartment. I tell him I have a friend living in Texas too, and I want to live close to her.

"I know it might not mean all that much to you now, Chantel," Dad says. "And I'm sorry I haven't been there for you to watch you get older, but I want you to know that I'm proud of you for everything you've accomplished, for the person you are today."

"I do know that, Dad," I respond. "Thanks."

A silence passes between us from one end of the line to the other, and for a time, we just listen to the other breathe. I watch the television screen across from me glare its bright colorful light, and I wait patiently for Dad to say anything else.

When he doesn't for five minutes straight, I ask if he's still there, and he says yes. "So, how are things going on your end?" I ask him.

He answers with a pleasant, "Fine," and asks how Alexis is doing in return. I tell him she's fine too, or should be, then explain that she's out of the apartment and living with Mom. She still hasn't read any of my messages or returned any of my calls, and I tell Dad that too. "Don't worry," he says. "I'm sure she will eventually. She can't shut you out forever, just the same as I couldn't do so with you. Eventually, she'll feel guilty just like I did, and she'll come back. You just have to be patient."

"Easy to say, harder to do," I reply almost immediately. I've heard that saying far too many times. It has begun to fade in meaning.

"I know," Dad says. "You just have to wait, and one day, God will bring her back."

It takes a while to get a reply out of me, but eventually I speak. "Sometimes I just feel like she has no reason to. She listens to Mom and Michelle more than she listens to me. She *believes* them more than she believes me. I don't know why. She isn't as smart as I want her to be."

"She'll grow into intelligence, Chantel," says Dad. "You need to trust that. You need to trust that God will make it happen. I know you haven't gone to church like you used to after finding out the truth about J.R., but will you pray for her?"

I think about that for a second, then nod even though he can't see me. "Sure," I reply. "I'll pray for her. I'll pray for her every night until Alexis decides to respond."

Dad is silent for a while, as if he's listening to the line, waiting for me to mutter that it's a lie or bullshit. After all, J.R. is a monster that God seemingly created for some reason, according to the Bible. Why would I pray after knowing what someone like *him* has done? This is

Alexis we're talking about now. I'd do anything to have her come back or talk to me again if she changes and sees the painful truth that I see. Otherwise, hell no, I'd rather live apart. I don't want her poisoned and brainwashed mind coming anywhere near me or my home, whether it's here in Kansas City or Houston, Texas.

"Thank you," Dad states in his usual soothing, deep voice. "Oh, and pray for your mother too, as well as Michelle and all of your family."

"For Mom?" I question. "Why? After what she has done for Roy and how she failed to protect her kids and grandkids, why would I?"

"Pray for her because she needs it right now," Dad explains.

"No kidding."

"So, why not?" he continues. "Pray that she'll eventually open her eyes and see the truth, that they all will. Pray for the victims that have been affected. And I know this is a stretch, but pray for J.R.—"

"For that monster too?! No way! I hope he goes to hell."

"In the hopes that he will change, Chantel," he finishes. "Pray for J.R. in the hopes that he will change."

I don't know if I should. I don't know if I want to. All that really matters to me are the victims that he has attacked. I want them to heal more than anyone else. It's all that ever mattered to me. They're the ones that I'm going to constantly be praying for, whether I have my faith in God or it lacks. The people who have been hurt under Mom's ignorance and J.R.'s persistence. I don't even know if I still believe in God's Word anymore after everything. The act of praying to God, hoping for better— I don't know how helpful it will be for Mom and Michelle and my Aunties or Roy. I don't know how helpful it'll be to Alexis. It's nice to think it will help, and I will pray for her, but will it change anything? I don't know.

I have to hope so.

I have to hope that, eventually, everything will work out. Whenever I'm ready to make my move elsewhere and start anew, all of this bullshit will be over and done with. Dad is right. I have to hope that it will get better, even if it looks like it never will. For the victims, and our family, and Alexis, Roy, and me. Even though I won't have Sabrina to turn to for guidance in Texas, I know I'll have Christina, Jessica, Dad, and who knows who else. That has to be enough.

"Okay," I say to him then. "I'll pray for them all. For Mom and J.R. and Michelle and Roy and Alexis. For all of our family and the victims combined. For our future. I'll pray."

"Great," Dad responded then as a hidden yawn revealed itself. I can tell he's smiling on his end of the line. "And I'll pray along with you."

Epilogue

I spend a day waiting for a call back from Patrick or anybody that works for the child services company. I don't hear anything. My phone doesn't ring from them again. That's really disappointing to me because this means so damn much to me, especially after Roy's anger outburst a week ago. If they don't get back to me I don't know what else to do.

It's crucial to spread awareness about matters like this. It's been avoided and ignored for far too long. Unusual sexual behaviors, abuse, and assault should not be swept under the rug. I've witnessed for myself the damage that it cause.

Another day passes. No response.

Then another and another, and eventually days turn into a week. So, I've started thinking about how else I want to break this pattern and continue to spread awareness to prevent it from happening again without the help of child services or the authorities. If they won't help me, fine, but I will find another way. I'll prove to Roy that he's wrong.

That's why I decided that I wanted to write a book on this matter, but not just any book. I wanted to write a book that shows the horrible occurrences that took place in my life and in my family. I wanted to shine light on what happened to us so it doesn't happen again. For the victims. For anybody, far and wide, that is even remotely involved. The fewer people speak on issues like this, the more dangerous this becomes and the easier it is for pedophiles like J.R. to take and to hurt again. The easier it is for them to get away with it. I won't stand for it.

My cell phone rings. *About time,* I think. It feels like I've been waiting forever. The caller ID indeed reads the number for the child services agency I called months ago. I pick it up at the end of the first ring.

"Hello, this is Chantel."

"Hi there, Chantel," says the same voice who I originally spoke to about all this. It's been a while since I've heard his voice. "It's Patrick. I'm calling for the report you filed with us. I understand you've been requesting an update for quite a while now. I apologize for the wait, but I finally do have an update for you."

"Yes," I reply. "Thank you. And?"

"We are indeed pushing further into an investigation with this file," he says, and that brings some relief to me. "We'll be interviewing the one you called J.R. as well as your mother and the children exposed within the next month or so. In doing so, we'll monitor their behaviors and responses to some of our pressing questions. We've been having quite a bit of difficulty. Your mother was very hesitant when we approached her. She wouldn't let anyone into her home, but myself and my coworkers are very concerned. We won't stop until this file is resolved, I assure you. Again, I want to thank you for bringing this to our attention. Is there anything else you need?"

I tell him no, that all sounds perfect, and I'm glad action is *finally* being taken. So with that settled, he says no problem and gives his standard "happy to help" mantra. Then we hang up and continue the rest of our days.

Later in the evening, I have a quick dinner in front of the TV and call it an early night. It's 7:57 p.m. I complete the day's journal as Sabrina suggested I do, and climb into bed with a deep tiredness.

I write today's date at the top of the empty page, October 11th. Then, I start with a brief and slightly vague recap of my day.

> *But what I find more disturbing is that Mom continues to keep that bastard around even while knowing he molested my brother. It's not like she's oblivious to what's happening, I don't believe she is. She knows exactly what's happening with Roy and Chad, all of her grandchildren, and she doesn't care. I hate that. I hate how she cares more about keeping a monster like him around when he's the one, in hindsight, that doesn't want her, but instead wants her children and grandchildren. It's sick. It's disgusting.*

I don't care about spelling or use of proper punctuation. I don't care about paragraphs. I just write it all in one. I write my heart out on the page, the pen scribbling as soon as I get through that very first sentence, and while it all pours out of me, I can't stop a single tear from falling down my cheek. It doesn't bother me. I keep writing, pouring my heart and soul into tonight's page until my hand cramps and I'm as good as done.

> *For my entire family to want to hide this and not stand for the victims of J.R.'s assault, it's disgusting and sloppy, and it just shows their character. Because family is your family, that doesn't mean they're good people. Mine aren't. I wish they were, but mine aren't. Integrity not only tells you who you are as a person but it shows your true character. I hate who Mom's true character is. I hate that Alexis is a follower of her too. Even though I tried to teach her better, really tried, she still doesn't like the fact that I reached out to do what's right and got Mom into trouble. It's dangerous to be a follower. It can lead her down a path to destruction, and I think that's what I'm honestly afraid of.*

I yawn, giving pause in my frenzied rush of rage-filled words. As tired as I am, I have to finish this journal entry, not because Sabrina told me to but because I just need to.

> *It's so much easier to be a follower. You don't even need to think. You can just do what everybody else is doing and not worry about the lives that are ruined by people like J.R.*

Ugh. The thought repulses me.

> *But I wonder… where would this world be if we only had followers? If nobody took the initiative to stand up and do the right thing? To protect those lives that really matter? Where would I be if I never chose to speak out or try?*

That's when I realize that my life will never truly be the same after going through this, how I wish it could be. Everything is so different now. It's changed so much, changed *me* so much but for the better. I smile at that, just slightly, not at the fact that any of this happened but at how better I am *because* it happened. It's like finding the good in a tornado of bad.

Another yawn escapes me and I return my journal to the bedside table at my left, along with the pen and I curl up under the covers to retreat to sleep.

I'm really hoping to dream of a fresh start, to dream of a better future where I am actively advocating for victims of sexual abuse more than I've ever been. I'm hoping to dream of relocating elsewhere away from my family hell. I want to dream of a better tomorrow under today's events. I want to hope that's possible at all.

I want what's better.

Coming Soon
TURNING TO NEW BEGINNINGS

My website: https://tewrites.com/

Instagram: @te.writes

REFERENCES

Ciccarelli, S., White, N. J., Fritzley, H. V., & Harrigan, T. (2015). *Psychology: An Exploration* (Canadian Edition). Pearson.

ColiNOOB. (2017). *Light bulbs* [Image]. Pixabay. https://pixabay.com/photos/light-light-bulbs-hope-glow-2156209/

Jotoya. (2020). *Kansas City skyline* [Image]. Pixabay. https://pixabay.com/photos/kansas-city-skyline-dusk-beautiful-5111825/

Nanavati, A. (2019). *Yellow brick road* [Image]. Unsplash. https://unsplash.com/photos/JYM97WANxcQ

Stoppler, M. (n.d.). *Facts you should know about healthy parenting*. Medicinenet. https://www.medicinenet.com/parenting/article.htm

www.ingramcontent.com/pod-product-compliance
Lightning Source LLC
Chambersburg PA
CBHW070043120526
44589CB00035B/2275